The power of tł

The power of the "PERSONA"

Do you know who you really are?

Roy Taylor

ISBN : 1-4196-1502-5

To order additional copies, please contact us.
BookSurge, LLC
www.booksurge.com
1-866-308-6235
orders@booksurge.com

The power of the "PERSONA"

Table of Contents

Special Thanks!

I wish to thank my ever-loving, loyal wife Sandy for her continuous love and support throughout our life and marriage together. This book is dedicated to our love and our relationship together over the years, may it continue forever!

Introduction

What Is It All About?

Have you ever wondered why you like one person more than another? What is it in their make-up that appeals more or less than another person? Sometimes it is not because they are particularly good or bad; it is not always governed by the fact they are thin or fat, good looking or not. It is an inexplicable magnetism that attracts people to become friends. You could argue that it is their personality, yes, personality, what is that all about? Were we born with personality or did we develop it as a part of our growing up in life?

I think that we were all born with a certain type of personality and that through the course of our childhood, we developed a way of molding ourselves to that personality. The thing is, just as we molded ourselves by incidents, relationships, and events in our childhood, we also developed other traits or mechanisms to protect ourselves from things we didn't like, or we developed ways to hide our innermost feelings from the outside world as a whole. It is in this part of our synthesis that we create the face that we put on to the world for our whole life and it is here that we create our "persona" that other people identify us by pretty much forever unless we make some fundamental changes along the road.

This "persona' is what I want to address through the coming pages and hopefully you will grow to share my thoughts on what it is all about and enrich your own life by the experience.

Going back to my early days of my childhood at school, I think I got this feeling about people before I met them and most times used that (intuition) to interact with them. Everyone gives off an aura of sorts; it is hard to explain, but if I put it in a tangible form, you probably will get my meaning better.

Imagine categorizing people into a temperature code or color code or into electrical charges (no I am not going crazy; give me a chance to complete the thought). In temperature terms, a warm person is a nice person to be around and a cool person has the tendency to make you a little uncomfortable or makes it feel like they are more difficult to approach. Now associate warm with orangey red for a color and positive for an electrical charge equivalent, and cool with dark blue, or negative for an equivalent electrical charge. I hope you are now getting my meaning. So when you are in someone's presence and you feel a little uncomfortable for some reason then they would be classified in the cool range or blue or negative. It is not as simple as that though people are not all in the extremes; some are more warm and orangey red than others and so you have to put them into a color spectrum of extremes or less extremes. The issue is, which side of the line are they? Then you have to determine how far across that line do they go.

Ok, so we have a method to measure a person's aura or "persona," so what is it about a person that makes up their 'persona"? Their personality certainly plays a part but there is more to it than that. What about their body language? That plays a major part of this equation also. What if a person is hunched over when they sit or walk or if they carry a smile or a frown, or if they never make eye contact, or they sit up straight with a superior air about them? These are some of the factors that make us draw judgment on whether we like a person or feel uncomfortable with them around.

We still have a way to go though. What about their appeal as a person? Some people have sex appeal and others don't, what is that about? A person with sex appeal does not have to be ravishingly beautiful and yet they make members of the opposite sex (usually) desire them physically. It is a phenomenon that people cannot buy or create; you either have it or you don't and whilst some learn to get close by their demeanor or actions, it is a gift. Nevertheless, it is certainly a part of one's "persona."

Sex appeal is usually derived from their sexual make-up as a person; in other words, it is rather like being a chocolate covered cream cake amongst muffins.

OK, so we have started to break down the make-up of a "persona;" what else contributes? How about emotions? This is another big contributor to this state of being and certainly needs to be looked at. Emotions are perhaps what can change a color rating from pale blue to dark blue or from pale yellow to orangey red. It depends upon the emotional make up of that person, I like to think

Controlling one's emotions plays a major role in how people perceive a person. Uncontrolled anger or joy can provide two different perceptions, as do withdrawn anti-social behavior and mild, polite quietness in the presence of others. Like jubilant outward demonstrations of happiness, any of these behavior patterns can greatly impact a third party who might be in the presence of such a person and to expand on that a little further; it can affect different people in different ways, some finding it pleasant or understandable—others finding it uncontrolled or ostentatious and strange.

Such is the complexity of the human spirit or "persona".

I have subconsciously or consciously analyzed and studied people my whole life and have found that fundamentally, most people do not pay a lot of attention to who they really are or why they are like they are. Most people either accept or don't accept the way they are and either live their lives covering up for it by withdrawing from the reality, whatever it may be, or alternatively, they become outwardly extrovert and loud as personalities in order to provide a barrier to prevent others from penetrating their vulnerability, thus putting these people most assuredly into the zone of the negative "personas." Obviously there are many, many more different personality types that can fit this category of person. For the purpose of this book, I am using a general description or analogy to help you to feel the example of my thoughts.

People who accept what they are usually have a deep faith in a higher power, are content with their lot and generally behave in a very warm and positive way in living their life. This does not automatically put them at the top of the scale, but it certainly puts them into the zone of the positive "personas." As I mentioned earlier in this chapter, you could have all things together as a person, but perhaps have a strange body image or disposition, which could detract from an otherwise perfect situation and consequently prevent you from being at the top sector of the warm zone.

To recap, it is not entirely what people do or say or believe or act like, it is also how they come across to others in their everyday lives, with family, friends, co-workers, and acquaintances, and how they perceive the person to be, however distant it may be from how they really are!

Let's ponder that thought for a minute. "People may perceive you to be different than you really are." That is a strong thought. How many times in your life have you been mistaken for being in a bad mood when you really aren't or been accused of being inconsiderate when really you weren't thinking in the present at the time, or perhaps you have been interrupting a conversation without realizing that you did in your eagerness to remember a thought? These are all actions that occur in our lives and we have no intentions of causing bad feelings, or upsetting anyone. This is often caused by emotions or by lack of emotions or lack of perception of a particular situation going on in our lives and greatly contributes to how our "persona" is viewed by a spouse or other person, if it is repeated more than once in a short period of time. It is the same as when outward displays of emotion affect the way people perceive one.

I hope that you now can grasp what I am trying to describe to you, and I hope even more that you are starting to think about what kind of a person you are in this picture. Well, don't try yet, o.k.? We have some more to cover before we go there.

I think that with the thoughts we have covered so far it is important to look further into what makes us accept the way we are, if we don't like what we see. There are so many things that mold our "persona" as we have already covered, but still we tend to accept that we are like that and live a life covering over the inner most mental pain and suffering. Even more than that, we allow it to affect our relationships. The kinds of things I am referring to are things that happened in our childhood: rape, molestation (heaven forbid the inexcusable sins and acts that they are) neglect, bullying, desertion, favoritism, verbal abuse, starvation, war, extremist religious indoctrination, bullying, poverty, obesity, anorexia—the list is shamefully never-ending. I am sure that I could carry on and list a lot more but my point here is that many of us have suffered these torments as children and adults and carry the scars within our very soul. They show on the surface and most definitely affect the color of our "persona" a great deal. Many times people hide these events inside and never share the pain they have and feel a sadness for themselves and this sadness shows in depression and a host of other side effects. People react to these things with anger, depression and shyness, low self esteem, failure at studies or work or life or relationships. They sometimes become promiscuous, take drugs, steal and kill as a result of their low self-esteem, and generally run in a groove like that and unless jolted from it, will stay there for the rest of their lives. There is no telling who handles what problem in what way; we are all different and we all have to find a way to continue with our lives after the event that potentially changed our direction for good. The problem is that we cannot go into reverse past the bad event or time frame and reset the direction on a better path and by-pass the problem. Wouldn't that be a great world to live in if we all could do that? There are several problems that occur with that thought; I think we might need a lot more time on this earth to get to where we might end up and secondly, good or bad, these trials and tribulations we have to suffer are stepping stones across the river of life and each one we cross makes us stronger and better qualified to handle future tribulations. I am not suggesting that there is any equality for any of us in the paths that we have to take through life, especially when it comes to comparison of life's experiences. But there certainly is a place of extreme peace at the end of it all.

Accepting that we are all different is an important part of the process of understanding that we need to work every living moment "to be the best person we can be, regardless of the burdens of life." Without effort, nothing really works properly and least of all the human "persona."

The negatives in our lives are the major contributing factors to the downside of life as a whole and if we could get a grasp on them collectively, I believe this world would be a far nicer place to live in.

The best portion of a good man's life is his little, nameless unremembered
Acts of kindness and LOVE.

William Wordsworth

This Book Is Dedicated To All Those Who Have A Cool/blue/negative "Persona" And Don't Know It!

Chapter 1

Relationships: Spouses And Significant Others

Now let us look at our relationship with our spouse or significant other. It is a very important part of our lives; at least it is for those that have a relationship. Those that don't have one need all the more to read this book. I think that fundamentally, people who have not had a meaningful relationship almost definitely have a low self-esteem or they have a selfish personality and consequently just can't get past one or the other and spend their lives wallowing in either or both.

There is a state of "persona' I call the Chameleon "Persona;" this is where the color of your "persona" is going to show its true colors at home and it may appear to be quite different to the one seen by our co-workers or friends outside in the every day living that we partake in.

I have observed many couples over my life and have found that it is possible for one party to have a different "persona" in a personal relationship than they might have for the outside world. It is particularly visible in relationships that have stood the test of time. Not all "personas" change but I think some do to adjust to the level of "persona" that one partner perceives they need to be, to live with the other. This does not always mean to please the other either, but rather means how they perceive they need to be in their relationship. For self-protection in a domineering relationship, it can mean complete capitulation sometimes to an overpowering spouse or it can simply be because they are taking the path of least resistance for an easy life with a spouse in a relationship that has grown stale, one that has gone to the lower extremes of cool or darker blue in color terms. This is not o.k. and needs to be remedied when present.

In addressing issues of warm and cool, instances and events in life can cause a "persona" to become warmer or cooler. The issue is that one must learn to recognize these changes and where appropriate, be able to turn things around and also be able to know the ways in which one can do it. There is no doubt that a cool or cooler "persona" is going to have a negative impact on the warmer "persona" and to that extent it will definitely have an impact on a relationship and if unchecked will eventually negate that relationship to no relationship or a very bad relationship. The overall aura around a relationship will glow very cool with this present. There is good news for even the weakest relationships, which can be made warm with selfless acts of unconditional LOVE so don't ever underestimate the powers available to you. Sometimes these acts may be responded to swiftly and in other relationships it may take longer; remember, if all else fails after repeated efforts on your part, there is always the "MEETING" (see below later). Remember, if you determine that you are turning cooler for whatever reasons that you make every effort to stop the cool trend and turn it around yourself, regardless of who is at fault for the trend. It is usually at least 50% you anyway and it is 100% your responsibility to make changes to improve things in a warmer more positive direction for your own good! Positive attracts and a warm "persona" will most definitely when exerted forcefully become the driving force in a relationship if consciously adhered to when negative forces normally would prevail. So be strong on these issues.

For example, you could be in a relationship where you feel that you are falling out of love with your spouse. This can be turned around by your taking a proactive role in the relationship by your instigating acts of unconditional LOVE. Initially you might not feel very loving but once this becomes a pattern in your life, your spouse will slowly come around to this way of thinking even if they were not before and the end result if continued will hopefully produce a much warmer more LOVING environment to cultivate the relationship not only back to an even keel but more importantly to a new level of positivity. . In a relationship where perhaps adultery has taken place, if you are the adulterer and your spouse is the innocent one and for whatever reasons you decided to QUIT, but you really could be persuaded to stay in the relationship if things were different, there are some basic rules. First, you have to truly apologize if they found out about it and if they didn't, then you must change your ways immediately, stop being selfish, make the commitment to perform lots of unconditional acts of LOVE and for sure, you must reinforce the relationship with your spouse in a wholehearted, honest, demonstration that is truly beyond question in any way, that means no more dishonest nights out under the disguise of work, no more card nights with the boys or what girls use as an excuse and exchange them with meaningful time with one's spouse. If you are a spouse who has been the victim of adultery and you have decided to forgive the errant behavior and your spouse has made this kind of promise to you, then you must truly find it in you to forgive the sin.

I know it is easier said than done, but it must happen no matter how long it takes, before healing can take place and, remember, if you don't forgive quickly enough, it may only serve as the final straw! It is so important to step back from your relationship and accept your spouse's faults as best as you can and not let them impact your "persona" in a negative way. There are many relationships that found a way to heal after such a devastating occurrence and it takes effort on both sides to make the cure and in addition to that, it takes even more maturity on both parts to dig out some of the root causes of the infidelity and try to fix them, so don't be afraid to investigate your innermost feelings and talk with your partner about theirs also.

When you discover that there are issues in your relationship that are causing it to make both your "personas" cool, it is your responsibility to attack the problem yourself, by making every effort to warm your own "persona" to the warmest orangey/red color that you can make it and become the leader. It really doesn't matter if your partner or spouse is the stronger character; you can be the controller of the "persona" temperatures in the relationship by instituting the necessary selfless acts of LOVE and tenderness that it takes to turn things around. Even the strongest of characters can be turned from a negative "persona" to a warmer "persona" when they are exposed to these positive stimuli. Your actions in the relationship can be very powerful. Cool is a demonstration of weakness; a cool "persona" really doesn't have control of their own "persona."

Warm "personas" generally have control of their "persona" and can also have control of "personas" in their sphere of contact, appealing to the "wanna be" part of cooler "personas" around them. It is really important to understand that and you have to work very hard at maintaining the depth of warmth of a warm "persona" and behavior patterns that warm "personas" need to live to in order to enrich these qualities. An example of an enrichment standard is as follows: let's imagine that you are a dominant type of person with a warm "persona" and one of the negative traits that stops you from becoming a really warm, glowing "persona" is that you tend to order people around you at home and at work to do things for the benefit of the home or work. Try changing that mode of operandum from order style leadership to request and suggestion style leadership. This could be simply demonstrated by going from, "you need to get your butt out of bed in the mornings" to "you know honey I sure enjoy the quiet time that we shared on Sunday morning when we got up and made a fresh pot of coffee and got to chat. I would like to do that more often, what do you think?" Softer yes, a little more time consuming yes, certainly gentler and more enticing and with out a doubt non-confrontational—just "WARM." This style of treatment of a partner will work wonders for you in your relationship. Don't give up if it doesn't work the first time. Stay with it. This inspires and motivates and ultimately will warm even the cooler relationships. So be respectful and polite and it will come back and reward you multi-fold.

It is not a major imposition for you to put yourself out a little, my wife has an endearing way of always making a pot of tea in the morning and there is never a morning that she fails to put a big hot mug of tea next to me while I am mentally preparing myself for the trials of the day. I just think that epitomizes what I am conveying to you about selfless acts of unconditional LOVE. In return I always try to make sure that little jobs around the home get taken care of in an efficient and timely manner. Do this kind of thing in other parts of your everyday life as a couple and let me tell you, life will become pretty good. If your spouse is burdened with too many tasks around the home, then help out. There is no paid chain of command here; it is a relationship of equality and if that is unbalanced in either one's perception, it will cool the "personas." Whining about this or that being their job around the home just does not cut it!

Start today and don't count the cost; in other words, just become that kind of person right now and don't change direction under any circumstances. Your life will glow by the response you get from everyone in your sphere of influence, period!

Try to attack family and household projects as a team, using each other's strengths to achieve the end result. It works and remember don't be judgmental of the other person; be praiseful and enjoy the pleasure of the experience. Like a great breakfast, it will set you up for a wonderful warm day (figuratively speaking) every day. Just remember, there are going to be negative events that take place in every day and most times they are instigated by negative "personas" who know no better. Learn to surf over them and continue to aspire to ride the wave of life as a warm, positive orangey red "persona." It will be an unbelievably good thing in your relationships with spouses, family, and friends.

This point I think depicts the statement entirely: a lazy person is a negative "persona" and I don't know anyone who just can't wait to be around a person who can't get their butt off the couch. They just aren't appealing, because others do not wish to perceive themselves in the same role unless of course they are one of them anyway. In my experience of life, I have always been able to motivate people to do unusually exciting things by doing unpredictable and fun things. I will give you an example of this kind of behavior.

One Friday night my wife and I were at home, our three kids were young and to find enjoyment and a source of entertainment, we invited another couple who were friends of ours to come over and play some board game and bring their kids over. We could bed them down with our kids and thus the parents could have some fun while performing the role of baby sitters as caring loving parents.

During the course of the evening while devouring a pizza, we all got to talking about how nice it would be to go up to the mountains a couple of hours away and rent a cabin and take all the kids up to the snow for some winter fun. My mind was just burning with warm thoughts about such an idea and knowing that the idea would be long gone by next week I suggested going that night. Well you could see the expressions on everyone's faces. First the women said absolutely crazy, and then the other wife's husband said not a bad idea but maybe we should plan it. I responded, what exactly was the problem, we all had a free time the weekend ahead. I knew someone who had a cabin and we could all pack the gear in an hour or so and be on our way. The women were excited but still offered resistance, which was crushed when I called the person with the cabin who said yes we could rent it for the weekend at a really cheap price. The decision was made, the kids were woken up, and I went to the supermarket with the other husband and bought essentials for the trip. After we had all gotten our gear packed in the two cars, we were on our way to the mountains at 10.00 PM that night and let me say, that was a weekend we all remember including each and every child. It was fun, it was cheap, it was spontaneous, and it provided huge amounts of kindling to the warmth of all "personas" involved and the many other experiences we have had since. Don't underrate the power of surprise and spontaneity in a relationship. Your spouse may resist any thoughts like this, ignore all resistance, throw caution to the wind and have fun in your life go with your heart all will benefit in the long run.

I want to take a moment here to emphasize something to you and I feel that you need to understand how I live my own life. You probably think that with all these thoughts that I must really have it all together and life must be just great. Well let me say this, I don't always adhere to my own philosophies and I also don't always live to the best that I can be. I do, however, have an incredibly good marriage. We both have times in our lives when the cool influences of life as a whole can interfere with an otherwise very warm relationship. I am not sure that anyone can have it perfect- but what I am sure of is that without effort to consciously control the negative or cool influences in our lives we will fall into decline. As far as the way I live my life, I always try to show respect for my spouse and I always participate with her in household duties. We work as a team and that never changes. I think that we have installed into our lives some automatic check points which remain intact even when we are in what can be described as cruise control. Sometimes pressures in life seem overwhelming and we lose sight of the simple things that we need to do to make our relationship's bubble warm, but I still believe that if we install the most important check points and make our spouses understand the realities that we have to face, presented in a pleasant and amiable manner, that our spouses really want to help us to handle our problems as should we do for them.

I hope that you understand what I mean by check points. These are embedded standards of behavior that both partners adhere to over all issues that take place in life. They are basic standards of behavior that make it easier for both "personas" to maintain at least a standard of warmth above neutral that the "personas" can maintain even when in cruise control. The basic contributors are, respect, honesty, self control of all negative emotions to a level of reasonableness that would be acceptable to a normal human being, Team spirit and selflessness, understanding and awareness of the other spouse's needs, combined with numerous acts of unconditional LOVE and hugs and kisses. That's it!

These are basic standards of behavior required to maintain a level of warmth in a relationship that will surpass most others and probably will make it last forever if adhered to in a disciplined, embedded way.

Let's take a moment and think back to the early days of your relationship with your partner, to the times when courtship was the priority over all else and that newborn LOVE inside you was kindled to the very depths of your soul. (The feelings that boiled up inside you that made you feel that no one else would ever matter more to you than that person you were in a relationship with.)Do you remember those feelings? Weren't they so warm you couldn't touch them? Those feelings just flowed out to everyone you came in contact with and it was beautiful right? In most relationships that white hot glow usually cools somewhat over a period of time, for some sooner than others but generally speaking it occurs in most relationships and it is usually caused by a fundamental laziness in people that causes them to take things for granted and not feel that they need to do as much to keep the fire burning inside. The trouble is that many couples never make the effort to put this problem into check mode and attempt to rekindle the fire while it is still very much in a warm, burning mode, and of course once it is in a cool or negative state it becomes a much tougher challenge. The key to the whole issue of cooling is that you must learn to recognize the events that are causing the change and put them in check as soon as you observe the trend; the sooner you do that the better. As soon as you see or feel a change in the warmth of your "persona," you need to revert to courtship mode to rebuild the fire and sure enough it will help greatly with your partner without even making an issue at all. Many times I think that people feel let down in a relationship because they perceive their partner as dropping the ball and of course they are right; the problem is that it tends to cool the "persona" of the victim which emits over to the other partner who is cooling faster anyway and so eventually there is this tailspin cooling effect that sometimes goes beyond control of either party even though they really don't want it to go that way. Eventually they allow themselves to accept this type of coolness in their life or they just check out and move on to another partner. The sad part is that moving on to a new partner is not necessarily the real solution; the problem is that you have to find the power to go back to stage one in the courting mode and try to rebuild from there.

This is especially important where there are children involved as I am sure you are well aware. So, the benchmark in any relationship usually can be dated back to where it began and it is sometimes very important to hit the rewind button to put it back on track. No matter what relationship you have with your spouse or partner, you can always put in more and that is where we all need to go in order to be "the very best that we can be."

Now let us progress to your feelings for that person today: has anything changed? What do you think has changed? You need to analyze what it was that made you feel so wonderful about that other person that made you fall in LOVE in the first place. When you come up with an objective overview of what has changed you may find that it is the passing of time or possibly that you are not contributing the same energy into the relationship as you did when you were courting. Separate the "good" things from the "not so good" and decide why the not so good things are in the list at all. The "not so good" things are the jobs to be done list and they need to be looked at very carefully, I suspect that the "not so good" list is a picture of why a relationship has cooled off and has taken on a different level to where it originally was.

THE MEETING! Now ask your spouse or partner to be completely honest and observe the original feelings they had in the relationship and write down their own list. Please make sure that both of you make a commitment to each other to handle the results in a mature adult fashion. Once you both have two lists, exchange them as separate lists for good and not so good, keeping each one sealed until opened, with each other without explanations. Read and observe what is "good" first, discuss what is good in detail and further discuss how the list of goods could be maximized in your relationship; in other words, discuss what the ultimate good could be in each item on the list and commit to each other to try to achieve it.

Move on to the "not so good" list and open them both together. No outbursts, no matter what is on the list. Remember, this is what your spouse or partner feels to be a legitimate problem in his/her life with you, provided they have been honest. Next, in each list discuss which items are selfish in nature. Highlight them with, hopefully, mutual agreement on the items as to whether they are selfish in nature. This is not a one sided decision; it must be mutual and make every effort to have the other partner agree to make changes. Once a short list of non selfish items remain on the list accept them as a valid other reasons for a cooling of the relationship and jointly try to agree on possible fixes that could remove them from the list. If humanly possible do not criticize just try to make them right in the best way possible. As with a Mother and her children, you have to have unconditional LOVE in your relationship with your partner and that also has to be non judgmental LOVE at all times. Judge yourself first and try to maintain a LOVING warm, patient "persona" at all times. It always starts with you and you owe it yourself to be strict with the standards that you live to. Never settle for mediocrity in your life or your relationships. There is no place for mediocrity in a positive "persona".

Don't give up just because it isn't great right now. The other man's grass is not always greener and your own relationship can be greener by effort and by putting LOVE into it and taking away selfishness and immaturity from the basis that it may be founded on. If a partner doesn't demonstrate those qualities needed to make the marriage or partnership strong it may be necessary to go back into the courtship mode to strengthen up the relationship and heal the imperfections that might be starting to show up in it.

The courtship mode requires an extreme amount of self discipline to successfully implement at a later date in a relationship, but the effects can be powerful on both parties if implemented with a sincere desire to succeed.

It should include, planned dates, romantic dinners at home without children present. It should also include weekend getaways and surprise gifts delivered at times when least expected in other words the relationship is in effect reborn with all the experiences of the past being made a part of the new relationship with forgiveness where necessary and acceptance of all faults being made a part of the newly reborn bond. This is so strong a warmer, in a cooling relationship that it will totally warm both "personas" if there is a desire on both sides, if it is only one sided; much more work has to be done in the analysis of the not so good list in order for it to progress further and resolutions to commit to the cause of common good must be achieved first.

Retirement, if you want an enriched retirement with your spouse, then you need to start investing in it as soon as you become a meaningful couple, I missed out the word marriage there because so many live together first and it applies there also. Just because you have retired does not mean that life is over, on the contrary, with a strong, warm relationship two "personas" who have spent the years prior, building warmth into the relationship will find that it continues glowing deeper and deeper in warm color the longer they are together and this should be even better served by a retirement event in their lives, if selfishness is kept solidly in check. This is a time to grasp life, to do the things that have been previously prevented by a work curriculum and now it is time to seize the moment and do all the things that have previously been unattainable for both parties in the relationship

There is an old saying that makes me think about relationships: "You reap what you sow" I believe that there is a lot to be said in the "persona" that is impacted by that phrase, people create their own destinies in life and they also have a lot of control over their own "persona" in couples, it is demonstrated very clearly by the close environment that they live in. The "persona" is to some extent magnified and we perceive the "persona" of the other partner very closely and the tendency is for us to respond to that "persona" in a magnified way also. That is sometimes negative and it can also be positive, depending on the glow of the other party in that relationship. The problem is that negative or cool emissions may have the effect of causing strong reactions from a partner that otherwise might be overlooked in a friend when present in them. So in this micro environment of a relationship, we have to be cautious not to allow little everyday events or lack of them and energy emissions that we might normally overlook to become outsized negative or positive stimuli that might impact our "personas" and uncharacteristically taint them. An example of this might be a partner making a remark about how their Mother used to cook the best roast chicken dinner and the other partner responding to the comment by misinterpreting that it was criticism of their cooking. This can occur frequently especially in a fairly new relationship where the confidence has not been built enough to not only understand the innocence of it but also to understand that even if they meant it, it didn't mean that there was any insult meant to the other partner and of course if they did mean it, surf over it! Such is the complexity of the human relationship. The problem with this type of situation is that it demonstrates how a lack of sensitivity in a person can have a bad impact on another in the relationship and thus make a negative or cool emission that can be picked up by the other and start the spiral again.

I have mentioned selfishness on numerous occasions in this book and I want to reiterate how powerful this is in a relationship and how strongly it can take a hold of both "personas" and drive them to the depths of cool quite rapidly and unless checked can destroy the relationship entirely.

If a person is selfish by nature because they have never been any different before entering a relationship, beware it is not going to disappear for long unless they choose to control it. In the early stages of a relationship it can disappear almost completely, but as time goes on, it may well come back with a vengeance if the relationship is not aggressively cultivated on a daily basis. I have seen many examples of success in this area but I have also seen more cases of failure and it is demonstrated publicly with their friends and family with no conscience. In single people it is present before a relationship but simply because they are living single and no one else is important at the time, it is different however, to the one that has it in their make up and doesn't care how the selfishness impacts anyone in their sphere of contact. Enough said, make sure you know who you are marrying before you make the decision to marry them. If you know what they are then it is up to you to work out how to deal with it because it may come back to haunt you later.

Keep in mind what we are dealing with in this chapter, we are addressing the issues that undermine a relationship and the ways in which we can check those issues and turn the impact of those issues around and learn how to not only maintain the relationship but to improve it with time and effort thus helping our own "persona" to at least maintain a warm glow at all times.

In finishing this chapter I feel that I should address terms of endearment, they are significantly important and once a term has been established for a spouse or partner, it should be made exclusive and not shared with anyone else; it is emotionally negligent for a spouse to drop that choice of endearment which may have existed from the time of courtship. As unimportant as it may seem to one, it can be enormous to the other and a term of endearment is usually founded in the most intimate of times in a relationship, it is not to be underestimated and should be used as often as meaningful and liberally. It is a subtle statement that they are still number one and in terms of warming a "persona" to feel number one at all times is a significant stimulus to the warming effect. If you haven't ever used a significant term of endearment, wait until an intimate moment, if that person is special to you and use it to demonstrate your emotions towards them that is like the christening of the term and should be embedded in the relationship forever.

True LOVE is made up of all the good emotions that make a warm "persona" and it runs very deep, it is strong it embraces all the major check points that stabilize the relationship and it also has a built in cruise control for the warmth of the "personas" it is like an aura that envelopes the parties that are experiencing it and it is usually a good influence on all who perceive it in others. The "personas" that possess it, don't necessarily burn warm at the top of the spectrum because it is also impacted by their own individual "persona's" but no matter what "persona" each has, when true LOVE is present, they are always in the warm spectrum at one level or another. It pays to make the effort, because the positive effects of a truly LOVING relationship with numerous selfless acts of unconditional LOVE will impact your life in its entirety.

YOU BETTER BELIEVE IT!

Success in marriage does not come merely through finding the right mate, but through being the right mate.

Barnett Brickner

Chapter 2

Relationships: Parent Child

This is the place where I want to start you thinking about your relationships that have formulated your "Persona". Let's start with your parents. Many who read this book have already got a good strong relationship with their parents or parent or maybe if they have passed away, you will remember a good relationship with them. Others may not have those good, fond memories of their parents and some may have no memories at all if you were orphaned or adopted.

I want to first of all address memories of childhood; we need to first look at the actual experiences in your childhood and thereafter with your parents that may have made those experiences special. Maybe there were events that took place in your childhood that you shared with them, or maybe there were personal interrelationships on a one to one basis that made an impact on you. Whatever they were, I suspect that they were all born from LOVE. Yes LOVE. I highlighted that because I think that LOVE is a major shaper of your "persona;" If you have the ability to receive and give LOVE, you will find that your "persona" will certainly glow on the more positive or warm spectrum of "personas" and that is so powerful, it will make your life feel good as a whole.

The amount of LOVE that you have or are prepared to share really will determine how strong you glow and I think it covers many areas of your life also. At the moment I am focusing on your relationships and how you can try to influence them by what you give and receive in a relationship. The parent child relationship is our first experience in life of the feeling of warmth that is derived in both directions when there is a healthy, demand-free unconditional LOVE in a relationship. Under normal circumstances this is the ideal and when present, it forms an unbreakable bond that lasts forever, through good and bad times.

Let's take a look at that situation and evaluate what can be learned from it. Whether you had a great relationship or none at all, it doesn't affect what we are going to observe right here. What we can learn here is why we need to carry what we learn forward in our lives forever and hopefully we can make a special effort to act this way even if we don't initially feel it in our hearts to be that way. As I try to attack this subject objectively, I will draw on my own experiences and observations and as you read this book I want you to make a special effort to take breaks from the book and start looking deep into your own experiences and try to be objective with yourself about how your life has been affected by a relationship you have had with a parent. I have to say that this must be a blood parent, not an adoptive parent, which I will address later in this chapter.

I have to start with the relationship with one's mother. This is supposed to be the most pure of all relationships, for both a boy or a girl and it is born of GOD (it doesn't matter what religion you are; what does matter is that you have a belief in a higher power. Suffice it to say that a mother's LOVE is so strong that she would give up her own life to preserve that of her child and that is awesome isn't it? Can you imagine the depth of LOVE that one has to have to be able to give up one's life for another? After Jesus, I think the mother must stand second on the throne of LOVE. Keeping this thought, mothers as a whole because they are human take the role of motherhood in a thousand and one different ways. Some are soft, some are loving and warm, some are tough, some are dictatorial, some are disciplinarian, and I can go on and on. But through all of their differences, they all have a common bond: it is unconditional LOVE for their offspring. We need to analyze this because it can impact a "persona" in so many different ways. What do I mean by that?

LOVE alone does not make it automatic that all children become warm "personas;" it is when other factors come into play with it. For example, a relationship that is born of a mother who is a naturally cool or blue/negative persona will not automatically develop a warm persona in her child because LOVE is present. Quite the contrary, it may develop a similar type of persona even though there is LOVE present in vast quantities. The coolness of the persona of the mother serves to do exactly that to the relationship with her offspring and can lead to rivalries and a host of other issues later in life, especially for the offspring.

The issue is that I believe that an offspring is also born with an inherent burning desire to have a perfect Mother and by that I mean a Virgin Mary type of mother, one who is all forgiving, all loving in her being and attitude, and one who can turn a blind non-judging eye on all of the acts of her offspring. One who is there with a hug and a kiss at all times of need whether older or younger and never criticizes their offspring's actions in a demeaning way. Oh! Right, Taylor, you are in "cuckoo land" (an English term for being crazy). No I am really not. Stop for a minute and look at your childhood. If you did get that from your mother, you don't feel cheated; if you didn't in some way or all ways, then I bet you feel somewhat, or very, cheated inside even if you have learned to live with it. If you didn't have a parent then you may well be seething inside because of what you have missed and don't even realize it. I hope that you can feel that I am trying to get to the bottom of your "persona," you have to draw your own conclusions for yourself as I go along, and these are things that you couldn't change or control as a child and maybe even now and for certain they had a major influence in your present day "persona.".

What I do know, is that if you are a mother and you are reading my book, then you may be feeling upset right now because you'd like to be like that but life's pathways just don't make it easy for you to be that way. I completely sympathize with you and suggest that you not be hard on yourself. This is not the time to make judgments.. Now is the time to find out where the causes are that make us cool, negative/blue on the "persona" spectrum and until we know how to recognize the issues, we cannot look for a cure, so have faith and hang in with me. There is a glowing, burning, very bright light in this tunnel for those who go the distance.

My purpose in describing a perfect relationship between a mother and her children is to set a benchmark for all mothers to work from or should I say, be aware of what the benchmark is. Remember "it is how you play the game of life that counts;" in other words, aspire to be the best that you can be always." This standard will vary from person to person and from time to time, so you might find that you cannot always be kind or selfless in your relationship but maybe you can make a special effort to be a better you than you have been and reset the level there to be improved on in the future when you feel strong enough to handle the effort or when you feel that the positive effects of the early changes are making you feel better. I am a believer in taking big steps in this area, not small ones. The sooner big changes occur, the sooner big improvements happen in the relationship. Whining and moaning about why you can't change doesn't cut it. JUST DO IT NOW! By the way there are no trade offs; accept the errors of your ways and correct them. If an offspring is partially contributing to the problem or even wholeheartedly causing issues, be aware, somewhere inside they feel cheated and they are making you the mother pay for it and you may not even know why. If you have an adopted child and they are making your life hell, even though you have opened your heart and soul to them and they just won't show any respect or behave badly with drugs or crime or whatever, it may well be because they are all fired up inside that their real parents "got rid" of them. They may not even realize it but they are carrying pain that wants to explode out of them.

If this occurs in a blood relationship, it is probably based somewhere inside the household. Obviously there are other causes for problems between a mother and her offspring. Usually it will resort back to the mother's relationship with her child; remember, kids know no better than they are shown!

So what about the father? Here is a bundle of worms. Under ideal circumstances, a father can be in the third seat on the throne of LOVE or he can be the root cause of many household disturbances that can detract from that warm, wonderful, cozy depiction of a great upbringing in a child's mind. A father can display (if he chooses to) all of the warm LOVE that a mother is capable of; however, the make-up of the adult male is so influenced by his masculinity, that frequently it doesn't get shown like that of a mother. Consequently, the end result is that a father's LOVE can be misconstrued by a child as the father not having LOVE. If this suppression of inner feelings by a father exists, a child can perceive this not only in how the father shows his feelings to their mother but also in their own upbringing whilst it may not really be the case it can affect a young "persona" sometimes for the rest of their life so it needs to be watched and addressed by any fathers out there who do have difficulty in showing their true emotions.

A father's role can be not only the icing on the cake of a good strong family relationship, but it can be half of the ingredients also. Fatherhood handled just right takes the utmost maturity to be able to lead and guide the family on a path that ultimately will contribute a lot to the "persona" a young offspring may one day grow up to possess. The father is a role that has many caps; it is one of bread winner, it is pillar of strength to the family, it is final decision maker, after discussions with mother and kids (where appropriate) on the subject of decision. It is a role of leadership on all family issues in a truly balanced family environment, and most of all it is a role of fatherhood in all senses of the word, which involves the spiritual health of the family, the educational goal-setter for children, and the final administerer of discipline when needed. This role should be capped with the statement :- praise and reward-giver when particular achievements are attained that benefit the family as a whole or that individually advance a member of the family unit i.e.: when good grades are received at school, sporting achievements, chores are performed without request, clean bedroom, great meal etc. These are all very important contributions to a household and a family unit and can, when performed very well by a father, play an enormous role in shaping a "persona." It can also serve to warm a wife's "persona" greatly by its perfect implementation.

The absence of a father to a child is potentially devastating in my opinion and is inexcusable if the absence is caused by divorce or voluntary separation under most circumstances. Children also have a burning desire to have a "GREAT" father, one who they can LOVE, look up to, one who they can boast about and one who knows everything. Kids have simple tastes and desires. It is up to each and every one of us to try and fulfill their utmost dream and in doing so, even if we don't quite make it, we give them the warm memories that they will live with forever. It is in these memories that we embed them with a basis for their "persona" in the future.

Take some time on that one. It is really significant that you address your parents' relationship with you and if it was less than perfect, you need to find forgiveness for everything and LOVE them for what they did for you. Somewhere inside (no matter what you think) they loved you. It is extremely important that you not psychoanalyze why they are/ were the way they are/were. Just accept that they are your parents and that God will reward them for that. Keep it simple. It doesn't matter anymore after today. Bury any hard feelings and move on. It is you that matters and you who we are going to build a strong foundation in and you are the only thing that matters in this book. No one else matters except GOD and YOU.

In looking back, I have this to regret, that too often when I loved, I did not say so.

David Grayson

Chapter 3

Relationships: Parenting

Parents should observe their offspring for qualities that they might possess and encourage them to progress in that direction if it is what they enjoy and have an interest in. When they feel the direction being taken is challenging and they start to become disheartened, then parental strength should be available to encourage and motivate their performance for success in that endeavor, with parents always having the awareness of mind to realize when they are "flogging a dead horse" and to change direction if necessary. Children need to experiment with different interests always and to allow a child to participate in one thing to the exclusion of all else is also a way of stealing their childhood from them. Many times I have heard a parent say this is all my child is interested in and the child when asked the question by the parent validates the parental response, but the child may well enjoy that sport or hobby, but usually it is because the parent has a fixation on that interest and the child wishes to excel to enjoy the favors and accolades of that parent to attain importance in the family structure. Parents should always be aware of the big picture; tunnel vision is not as productive as some would imagine and sometimes deep within a sports success is a cool "persona" trying to get on to the warm side, and not really realizing why.

Parenting is a tough job, there are no hard and fast training programs and we all tend to follow a path that our parents followed with us, with modifications on things that we did or didn't like in our own upbringing, the problem is that because of the difficulties that all adults face in their life's struggles, the quality of parenting is enormously varied and thus the individual "personas" of every human being vary as enormously also. Where do solutions lie to this huge issue? There are many, but I think that if we all take the path of "being the very best that we can be" as our creed not only in life, but also in parenting, the lives of our children will all benefit, perfection is not an attainable goal, but effort in that direction is very doable and all parents need to keep clearly in focus that children need to be children and family togetherness is top priority. For those families that don't sit down to eat at least one meal a day, preferably the evening meal without the TV on, they should give it a try, it promotes warmth and group conversation about all subjects and it demonstrates the presence of LOVE in the household, use the opportunity while it can be used and even when children have grown up and moved out of the home, parents should still continue the tradition whenever possible.

Let's move on from the early years of childhood to teenagers. Girls and boys follow similar paths in their early years; maybe playing different games and mixing with their own gender, but once they start to notice the other sex, they start to really change directions in their growing up process. In puberty, this where their true "personas" can get disguised for several years, while they transition. It is a time when they are not only changing physically, but it is also a time when they generally become acutely aware of themselves almost in a microenvironment of selfishness. They are at a time when they are truly reaching out within themselves to find out who they are and where they are going in life. Teenagers are at their most vulnerable during this time, because they are open to any influence that influences their life, both good and bad and for many they are aware enough of their childhood values to discriminate between right and wrong. The problem is that for many others, there is the urge to branch out and make their own decisions in life and the temptations that are out there can be very appealing, especially if they are introduced by their peers. It is during this time of invincibility as they perceive it, that a warm or cool "persona" could almost be described as a neutral, because the real "persona" is so well disguised by other influences in their life, These can be drugs, bad music, gangs, sub cultural groups and of course a host of other negative influences which in most cases remain present temporarily disguising the true "persona" of that human being. Obviously these types of influences are potentially destructive permanently if not brought strongly into check by both parents with complete undivided focus on the issue or issues at hand. Parents sometimes feel that turning a "blind eye" on the issue will enable it to go away. Not so, in most cases it can potentially be very destructive and it needs more family support then than at any time in their childhood. Parents must enforce the family standards rigorously and impose penalties for any and all breaches of the household rules. Remember, the child already knows the family rules and which of the parents is the "soft touch" on serious issues and will use that knowledge to its fullest extent. The fact that a child becomes secretive or quiet or withdrawn is usually a statement that they are up to something that needs to be checked. No child's bedroom is secret from a parent and access to all children's belongings is a parent's prerogative at all times while they live in the household, even if they are over eighteen years old. I know that sounds awful but what is better: ignoring a child who is developing a bad habit or saving them before it develops any further?" Interrogation as to their whereabouts and activities and who their friends are, is ok. Even banning them from mixing with friends that are suspect is ok. Tough measures yes, what about their "persona?" At this age their "persona" is up for grabs by the devil and we cannot change our position about right and wrong in any way at this time in their lives, the child is watching you to see how strong you really are and if you LOVE them enough to fight for them and let me tell you, you gotta fight and fight to win o.k.

This does not always have to be like this if parental involvement exists strongly throughout a childhood and it is extra strong positively with, of course, lots of understanding during the teenage years with controlled relaxation of some rules at times when necessary. For example: : dating (supervised initially) dances (chaperoned) in other words, allow natural progression but never without parental influence and curfew being stringently enforced even into late teens. When I say curfew I mean ten o'clock for boys and girls through twelve years old at any event and 10.30 through sixteen years of age and 11.00 until they pass twenty-one years old. You might think that is archaic but it is necessary if you want to control the negative events that can occur in a child's life after dark. I stress that even with a curfew, knowledge of where they are and a phone call from the child should be mandated if any changes of plan occur. Please note, this does not guarantee success but it sure will help with the majority in the battle.

The involvement that a child experiences from a parent will definitely help when they hit this period of teenagerhood in their lives and hopefully the need to get kicks elsewhere will be suppressed. When it comes to girls and boys I think that the actions I have suggested above would apply to both the same, if parents do not apply LOVING strategies to protect their children, then the inevitable can often become the reality and the issue of a warm or cool "persona" is not an issue at all it can have the impact of a sledge hammer on a child's "persona" in the negative or cool direction. I am not suggesting that all children are the same at this time in their life because of parental neglect, because even with the strongest positive parental involvement some children still go on their own path, usually it is because they have become devious enough to fool even the most diligent parent. The key though, is to respond at the first instance that the problem is recognized no matter how tough the confrontation and not turn away because of what might happen in a confrontation.

What I have discussed above is not to be confused with the following syndrome that appears to happen in most households where children are reaching out for maturity; it is usually more dramatic in boys than girls but nevertheless most go through it. This is the time when a child decides that they have fully grown up and can handle their own life and doesn't need any parental influence at all. For some parents this can be devastating and for others it can play havoc around the family home while it exists. In boys, they do it by deliberately flaunting house rules and guidelines and usually if a father is present, it is up to the father to hold rigid on the rules of the house at all costs. The reason for this is that if the father bends on this, there is a loss of respect by the child and the dominance in the home can be perceived as passed over by the child which could lead to further breaches and acts of household dominance that are not positive under any circumstances. The issue is that the occurrences when they happen are to be recognized as gestures of wanting to spread their wings and find their own independence and while a position of strength is demonstrated in the household, a position of understanding the need in the child must also be recognized. Once this is achieved, the parents need to offer a solution that is possibly in the short term or if not feasible for whatever reason, a long term plan with some minor concessions made to appease the situation from a negative decline.

To restate this period of teenager-hood and where it impacts a "persona" one has to recognize the turbulence in a child's life during this period and not to automatically assume that they now know better and can decide for themselves. This is not true and yes they can make decisions but with parental guidance and assistance, so we must not take it for granted that an old head is on young large developed shoulders and body. So often the true "persona" of a teen growing through puberty and late childhood is tucked away in hiding, but rest assured if the wrong influences are present during this time, it can certainly affect their "persona" in a negative or cool way. Just the same in a positive or warm way if involvement in community or personally rewarding activities is encouraged and cultivated, so it is not a time for parents to quit; on the contrary, it is a time for seizing aggressively with lots of positive stimuli that may be mutually rewarding for both parent and child, or at the least, rewarding for the child. Parental reward can sometimes come from watching a child benefit from an experience.

In finishing this chapter on children and the parental influence in a child's life, it cannot be overstated how important the relationship both parents have with their child affects the child's "persona" and how the lack of involvement can be potentially devastating if the neglect is ongoing and plainly obvious.

Children: take care of them, they are precious like little flowers and they need to be nurtured, LOVED and tended often.

Roy Taylor

Chapter 4

Relationships: Siblings and Children

How about one's brothers and sisters? Where do they fit into this "persona" that we all have? They all play a big part in it also; they are one's partners in life forever and can be hugely influential as they can be both positive or warm or orangey/red in one's life, just as they can be cool or negative/blue in one's life. The problem is that they are around from a very early age in your life and they share so many of the early experiences. Even though they share our childhood, they still grow up with different "personas" and for all that we have discussed so far you would think that they would at least have similar ones anyway. Not so. Many of course possess similarities in their "personas" but in reality the "persona" is only guided by our relationships. It is not controlled by them. Also, the relationships that one sibling has with a parent can be quite different than that of another sibling and that same parent. The thing that really is important with siblings is that there is a bond that is born from blood usually and it is one that should in its perfect state be one of unconditional LOVE and trust at all times. Anything less is not an acceptable standard. Read that again: anything less is not an acceptable standard.

Too many times this is a relationship where that old satanic monster creeps into a family unit and it is called JEALOUSY! What a destructive emotion that is. It can destroy even the best of potential relationships as and when it pops its ugly head up. We will be dealing with couples and their relationships later and of course this monster comes out there also. In siblings, it can occur as a result of one getting more attention than another or because the other one is around, period. Most of the time it starts off in a simple basic form and then, like a cancer, it embeds itself into their "persona" and there it festers and grows and unless it is controlled by the person who is inflicted with it, it can destroy them to a point that their "persona" is so cold and dark blue, that no one can stand to be in their company. This is very common with siblings and it is often created unwittingly when a parent favors one sibling over another. In a family there should never be favorites of any kind. Yes attention when appropriate, but dished out equally no matter what the excuse.

Sometimes siblings are born of different academic or artistic abilities and it can happen that if one shines in an area where a parent has a particular interest, they can inadvertently get much of that parent's attention. Or if one particular sibling is particularly involved in a demanding activity that requires much parental attention, or if one sibling has an unusually extroverted personality and consequently they get the center of the floor on all major get-togethers with other family members or friends—these are instances that can drive other siblings to compete and this may result in misbehavior or attention-getting acts that are construed as annoying by unobservant parents. The other extreme of this can be introverted behavior or shutting themselves away from the other family members living in their own world of escape, because they are feeling pain and don't know how to deal with it. It is all a form of jealousy. In a family situation it is generated usually by others taking them for granted and not paying attention to the fact that they have feelings and need attention also. The trouble is that it is often a simmering volcano being created for future life and to say that it is "persona" impacting is a fair statement and should be watched for in all youngsters, because it can be caught and fixed at an early age.

While on this subject, I want to point out that if siblings are brought together from different families, many fatal mistakes may occur here. But they can be checked at the door if handled correctly. I am digressing a little because I think that this is a really significant "persona" influence that rarely gets a lot of attention in relationships.

Where a child or sibling is put into a new relationship and one of their blood parents is no longer in their daily routines, this is a potentially devastating event in a child's life. It is so important that the parental influence, both old and new, maintain a mature stance to handle the situation in the best way possible, which includes not being overly passionate in the young person's presence. It involves the new parental influence making gentle but obvious moves to involve the child in his /her sphere of activity and interest and it also involves making a very special effort to make the child feel that the departed parent or blood parent who is no longer present on a daily basis is talked well of regardless of his/her sins. I always think the word "step" in step-child is one of the most undermining titles that there is in any parental relationship and should be expunged from the English language. What a downer that is to a relationship. Just think what being called a "STEP" son or daughter can feel like a second-class citizen maybe? If you are the victim of that misnomer I LOVE you and forgive them for they know not what they do! I agree that an adult may not think that a child should call a new dad or mom by that name because they aren't in the blood sense, but to a child, that is exactly how they see them, no matter what you tell them and they are trying hard in their little hearts to find a way to please their mom or dad in case s/he leaves also. They are trying to make friends and find LOVE for that person she LOVES now and sometimes a fight is going on inside because they really don't want the new change in family structure.

I am not advocating shoving it down a child's throat, but I am suggesting that a child should always be allowed to make the decision what they choose to call a new dad or mom in his/her life. It can do no harm. Hard as it sounds, it is the quintessential act of a real father or mother who has "QUIT" the relationship to step back and allow a Daddy Dave or Mommy Sue to come into the picture without all the selfish, childish undertones that go with the split up. Remember the blood one is always Dad or Mom with no other add-ons.

I thought that this was a good time to address that issue because I think DIVORCE is the other satanic demon in the world today that other than jealousy can affect not only offspring in their relationships but also couples in theirs.

Remember this is not a book of criticism, it is a book of observation and the intent is to help you to observe your own "persona" and family members and friends and life's experiences, as well as how you relate with them and how you can improve your own "persona" in the process of becoming a more observant person and becoming more aware of how your "persona" affects others around you.

Ah! yes, the "persona" is self driven inside each and every being and it is that delicate balance of mind, body, relationships, aspirations, and expectations mingled with life and all its experiences that plays a significant role in how the "persona" glows. We need to understand that in order to progress to a higher level in our life, which we need to not just accept our lot, but to accept our faults also and make a goal to change them on a daily basis in a new refreshed mind set.

In the last chapter, we dealt with some of the influences that a parent can have on his/her offspring and the impact that neglectful or non-existent, unmindful acts can have on the warmth of a person growing up in the world. In this chapter we will examine some basic child upbringing events that should be adhered to very strongly.

Firstly I must address the issue of discipline in a home. Today, there is an enormous change in the way parents raise their children than when I was raised. I think that whatever way a child is raised inside the family group, there is a need for guidelines of behavioral standards and there needs to be reward for adherence and some form of reprimand for non-compliance. All children at some point test the perimeters to find out if there are any areas of breach that can be found without any consequences, and that is normal. However, it is not good for a parent to allow a child to break the household guidelines of behavior unchecked. The determination of how severe the offense lies with the parents, and how the punishment is administered is equally important. In many families the administering of discipline is where the first instances of cooling in a child's "persona" take place. For example if one sibling is punished differently than another or punishment is administered more frequently than would be determined as reasonable by a normal person. On the other side of that coin, there is also the issue of not enough parental control being influenced on a child's behavior; this can also impact a child's "persona" in a cool/negative way. How? A lack of disciplinary adherence in a child can cause others to treat them in a negative way, by ignoring them, speaking badly of them in their presence, and generally making them unpleasant to be around. So often the parents are totally blinded by their LOVE of the child that they don't see it.

It is important to maintain standards of behavior a child should live by in the home and also outside of the home and with gentle checking varying to stronger enforcement depending on the offense and whether it was a mistake or deliberate disobedience. Having said that, I think that all children need to have a set of standards to live by; it makes them better, more acceptable members of society and it also makes them more cognizant of what is accepted in society as normal behavior. Tantrums, such as biting, spitting, answering back, swearing, cheating, and lying, should never be left unchecked. These are NO-NO's in life and are issues that if left unchecked, lead to some form of selfishness and other anti-social traits in a human being. First time around a warning is in order, then a disciplinary act if it is repeated. Too many times I have heard parents, both mothers and fathers, issue a warning and then warning after warning, with no follow through. Guess what? The child now knows who is in command! A child finds security inside a set of life's guidelines set by their parents and that perimeter around them needs to be kept strong. It serves to promote warmth in a child's "persona."

There are many influences that affect a child's "persona" development and during the next few paragraphs of this chapter, I'll outline some issues that I believe can impact a child into their adulthood in such a strong way that their ultimate warmth as a "persona" can be rooted right from here.

Let's start our thought pattern on the things that have an impact in a child's life. First of all is LOVE. This is the number one ingredient that needs to be present in all aspects of a child's life. For example, if you have ever had a puppy in your home, you remember the innocence of a puppy and how it's life is all play and how it shows its LOVE by jumping all over anyone who cares to give it affection in even the smallest way.

I remember that so clearly and I think that is why people LOVE puppies and children; they share the same innocence towards everyone around them and all is great until the day you are out walking your young puppy that may have grown a little from his very early youth and innocently he/she barks and wants to play. The puppy barks at the dog coming down the street that is not on his leash that has no intention of playing but wants to exert his influence on the puppy and comes over to make trouble for him. The puppy in his innocence jumps up at the dog and then it happens the dog starts a fight and bites the puppy who gets hurt; you beat the big bully off and take the yelping puppy back to the house to treat his wound. To finish off my analogy, the puppy is now changed forever; he no longer trusts other dogs and even becomes aggressive himself as a defense mechanism. Children do the same thing when a parent or LOVED one lets them down or abuses them and they change a little or a lot each time cool or negative things like that happen to them. Issues that affect children vary greatly and parents need to be aware of what kinds of things in every day life can harm a child's mind and make them build coolness into their "personas."

Parents arguing in a child's presence, a parent bad-mouthing the other parent to another in front of the child, separation for good or bad reasons. Neglect, by lack of attention, lack of interest, fatigue, by self-indulgence, lack of presence, all of these issues of neglect can play a role in "persona" cooling. You can liken every bad incident in a child's life as a scar and each scar growing tissue of negative ness into that "persona". It doesn't take much to develop a pretty cool "persona" in a young adult if their childhood has been inundated with little "scar" events. Parents who handle their own problems publicly around the home for children to view is an extremely tough thing for a child to handle in their little minds, they blame themselves for Mommy or Daddy's upset or anger or misery, this they should never have to deal with in any time or place at an early age in life when to the best possible way, everything should be rosy around them or at least appear that way.

A child was not made to grow up immediately they can walk. Like a bird, they need to obtain nourishment and shelter from their parents until they can fly and even after that, strong parental involvement means that it was all more than just a chore to the parents, it was an act of LOVE emancipated by numerous acts of unconditional LOVE.

There are some things in a childhood upbringing that children hold very dear if allowed to do so, they are enormously powerful influences in their "personas" and in my opinion should be implemented aggressively by parents always. What I am referring to is happy time celebrations, Birthdays, Christmas, Santa Clause, Tooth Fairy, Thanksgiving, Confirmation, Graduation, Recitals, Plays at School, Open House at School. These are happy time moments if handled right by the parent and rest assured they carry enormous amounts of white hot warmth additive to a child's developing "persona".

I said if handled right in the previous paragraph and I should like to dwell on some of these occasions to show what I find relevant in them. I did mention a couple of religious holidays in the list and I should like to add that if you are of a religion that celebrates other occasions in your religious calendar and it is something that a child can get excited about, then add it to the list, but only if it is fun. If your religion doesn't have a particularly fun celebration occasion in its calendar, then give Christmas a break and get into the spirit of it even if you don't believe in the story and event. Stay with me on this, it is important for the children. Children don't know what they want to believe about religion; they just want to enjoy the happiness that goes with it.

So let's go to birthday. Any birthday is good but that of the child is the most important bar none and needs to be given that priority status. The birthday celebration must start when they wake up and finish when they go to bed.

It goes something like this: decorations around the home for them to walk into when they get out of bed, their choice of breakfast, if it is a school day, wear their favorite clothes or a new outfit if the budget allows. When they come home from school a party is arranged and if possible their favorite friends and people present, a cake must be there with their name on it and balloons and music and games and happy fun things until bedtime. That is a birthday celebration and should be followed through with obvious variations according to age, through their whole childhood.

Now Christmas, what a wonderful time of the year. For younger children it should start with an advent calendar on the first of December and a little door on the calendar should be opened by the child each day when they get up in the morning or when they get home from school with a little token reward or candy to celebrate each door opening in the calendar. For those that have not done this before, behind each door there is a picture of a scene from the events leading to the birth of Christ and the last door is on the 24th December when Christ was born. From a child's perspective the pleasure is derived from opening the doors and seeing what picture was behind the door and each day they will be excited to do it. Then there is the decorating of the Christmas tree and all children should be allowed to participate in this process along with the whole family playing their role in the decorating process. Note this should take place at least two or three weeks before Christmas, not more than that because the excitement must remain for the whole time. For a child, this is one of the most magical times of the year if handled with consideration for what it represents to the child by their parents. Christmas music should be played at regular intervals when the children are present, even the older ones should be exposed to the joyous season of "goodwill to all men and women," leading up to Christmas day and especially during the dressing of the tree. The Christmas feast should be what makes you happy, but it should be a "Feast" and the children should enjoy treats that they don't get any other time of the year. It adds to the magic of the occasion.

Now we move on to one of my favorite events at Christmas, "Santa Clause." This is I think one of the most magical moments of the whole year for children that are privileged enough to enjoy it and I think children should undergo the full nine yards on this event milk, cookies, early to bed and comments prior to bed time about, "I thought I saw Rudolf pass the window just then, did you see him? Let's take a look." This is so important to a child if it is possible to have it happen. I have performed this role for literally thousands of underprivileged and privileged children and let me tell you, they are all the same when it comes to Santa. Parents, I must say this to all of you that read this book, do not let Santa go until the child is nine or ten years old, even if they tell you they don't believe in him, as long as you hold on to it and don't admit anything, when they pass six or seven, because you don't let it go and their friends tell them otherwise they still hang on with you a little bit and we need to grasp every little vestige from the experience.

Why? Because they are kids and they need to remain kids as long as we can let them be that way and that means not making fun of Santa when they are in the seven to ten age brackets. There is plenty of time to be adults.

The Tooth Fairy is next and if possible every time the child loses a tooth it gets put under the pillow and is replaced in the night by the parent with a quarter or a dollar. It is not the amount; it is the event that counts. There are parents who don't do it at all and some who don't get it and do it wrong; it is for the children and the well being of the family that it is good and should not be undersold. The same applies to the other celebrations during the year and their importance needs to be explained on each occasion. I will finalize on the subject of occasions at school. These are very important to a child and my heart goes out to any child whose parents are so wrapped up in their own lives that they cannot find a way to break away and attend a special event in their child's life.

If you go, make sure that there is lots of praise given and if the child is struggling with their school work, find out how you can help them to succeed. It really matters. Again, this is where the warmth of a "persona" is cultivated and it really counts.

While I am on the subject of warming children's "personas," I think it prudent to mention other things that can contribute greatly to their warmth and your own also at the same time. Find good things to do together as a family or as a team, like camping, fishing, movies, park, beach etc. these are all wonderful in their own right, and need to be enjoyed at as many occasions as possible and if you can, calendar them in advance so that they can be looked forward to for weeks or months it adds to the anticipation and will never be forgotten. If any event is planned with a child involved in it, the parent must make it a major part of the plan to involve the child in their activities, so the activities must have a youthful flavor to them, not going camping and ignoring the kids once you are there o.k. If you do something like camping, it doesn't hurt to bring a friend of the child's with you. It will do them a favor and your own child will have even more fun having a friend come along and who knows the other child may also benefit greatly from being involved in a warm family experience.

Childhood is so special and parents should make every effort to allow children to be children; to steal that from them is a bad error on the part of any adult. Children need their childhood to formulate their true identity as a person and if wrongly influenced by a parent or parents then the child's "persona" risks being developed by that loss. This will override their natural growth and the end result is an adult who may be strongly blue and either locked into immaturity until a life's experience changes it, or they may never shake it at all and remain an immature adult forever. It is harmful to play with nature and where children are concerned; we all need to understand that we are playing with fire when we steal such a wonderful thing away from any child.

There was a quote in a parable in the bible that stated words that read "look at the world through the eyes of a child." I hope you know why that phrase was coined, it was because innocence is at its purest in a child and we need to respect that and cherish it as long as we can. Any parental acceleration of that natural process of growing up is really an act of selfishness on the parents' part. It is not a benefit in any way for a child to be force-reared to become an early adult. The life a child should enjoy in their early days is one of worry-free, carefree time preferably with their mother in a setting where they are the center of attention. This promotes all the warm good things a child needs to grow up into the world. Gently along this path they need to broaden their awareness of the world and its good and bad things, whilst still under the mindful eyes of their parents. Children should be cherished and nurtured at all stages of their growth not in a suffocating way, but in an encouraging, LOVING way so that they can gently expand their own horizons at their own pace.

One of the events in a child's life which has an impact on them in the formation of their "persona" is when they become involved with sports. Most parents involve their children in sports for all the right reasons, learning sportsmanship, team spirit, exercise, motor skills, and this can very quickly become a parental thing in which the child is soon relegated to second position after the parents find a reason to deal with all their own issues inside, they try to make the child play to their own level that they played to as a child and the child may not be able to and thus their life is made a misery by the domineering parent, or a parent may push a child to attain a level that they could not reach themselves as a child and the child is made to feel like a failure because, like the parent they are not that good at this activity themselves either. Parents can display the most disgraceful traits of how not to behave, unsportsmanlike acts of verbal and physical abuse of other parents and children, demonstrations of "winning is the only thing that is important not how you play the game," sure winning is fun and should be applauded, but if losing has to happen, it is not something to be ashamed of as long as you did your best! In life, we all have to suffer losses and in my own life there have been many, would I have chosen to miss them out of my life of course, but then my inner most soul says NO! Why, well my best learning experiences have come from the times when I am at my worst loss and for that, I have to thank God for putting me in a place where my vision is at it's best and my perception is clearest, so loss is not necessarily the worst thing that can happen even as some parents that I have observed would have their child think. Loss can bring a strong resolve for success and regardless of what some parents think, inside their child is an understanding that they learn from their peers, that winning is good and can be fun. The trouble is that sports for some parents often changes from their own child's development to a situation where they attempt to vent their own weaknesses and failings in a platform that is really the child's domain what a shame.

Where there is LOVE there is life.

Mahatma Gandhi

Chapter5

Relationships: The Past

When a person has a dark event in their past that they hang on to without sometimes even realizing it, they live their life around that event in every moment of their life and, for whatever reason, they react to other people with that particular event as the basis or foundation of their relationship. Consequently, they create a basic flaw in their ability to relate with not only that person but everyone else they relate with in their lives. So they grow up in life but never mature past that event. This happens with millions of people in as many ways, in varying degrees of intensity. They carry forward with them parts of their childhood or early adulthood and just cannot let go. Some know what it is and others don't but either way it can be an unbearable weight on their shoulders and for their emotional psyche.

I want to pictorialise this thought for you; envision carrying a fifty pound sack full of old sharp bits of steel on your back up a steep long road for fifty miles (this is the burden we carry of a bad experience from the past during our life), then imagine carrying a ten pound bag of soft wool on your back for ten miles of that journey to rest your head on when you took breaks (this is the good wholesome relationship without the burdens from the past) in addition to the fifty pounds of steel Which would you rather do? Yes the wool sounds really appealing right now, but imagine what your mental disposition would be like during and at the end of the journey if nothing changes. Yes, you've got it, you wouldn't want to add the burden of the wool bag if you still had the bag of steel even if it was for a short distance. It would be just too much and you would feel cheated of the head rest, right? Well that's what it is like in life. If you don't find a way to shed the burden of the past (the bag of sharp steel), good relationships won't happen and last (you won't be able to carry the extra bag of wool).

Pursuing this on a more positive personality, I have found that people who are generous in their soul, with their time and their riches (big or small) are warm people. I have also found that people who are modest are warm people. The people who find the ability to see humor even in tough times are usually warm. Those who are willing to accept their lot, without complaint, are also. Ah! Complaint, there is a big one. I think that complainers are so cool and negative; they drive any "persona" down about two or three notches on the color scale every time you are in their presence. Why? Because, they impact the "persona" of everyone in their company at any time they start.

It is really important to realize that a negative "persona" will, nine out of ten times, lower the warm glow factor of a positive "persona" when in their company, thus providing a less than optimum atmosphere when they are present in company. Should a negative "persona" be in the company of another negative "persona" it will have the effect of a ghost being in the room. Yes, it will provide a very cool/chilly environment, one to be avoided wherever possible! You need to be aware of these "personas' if you wish to improve your own and you need to find ways to handle them when in their company; if they happen to be a spouse, family member, or close friend, you definitely need to have a plan of defense.

I have found that people who have found real maturity usually have the gift of a warm, positive "persona;" they're the kind of person who in their life's ordeals has found a place where they can handle life in such a manner that even the toughest ordeals are kept within their sphere of control. They're able to relate with others regardless of their tribulations or past events and still emulate a warm and positive "persona." These are truly some of the warmest people. This is not an intelligence thing, nor is it a success financially thing; however, it can embrace both those if all the other things are present that create that warm, positive "Persona."

In personal relationships, most of us find that there are times when the other spouse or significant other, have their off days (some more than others!) as we do. The real issue becomes when they allow more off days than good days to dominate the relationship. You notice that I said when they allow. Yes, I meant that. I think we should all be empowered to work at the best relationship that we can have with any person that we make a promise to be a partner with; that applies to work and home.

On off days in a relationship, many of us tend to get tunnel vision and adopt a very selfish attitude to their solution. In other words, we tend to provide resistance to the other's drop in warmth level by reacting aggressively or negatively, rather than introducing a positive or warm stimulus to the situation.

So personal relationships don't just happen and they don't stay the way they are; they tend to trend with the cooler of the two "personas" in a household and that generally will continue to slide to a darker blue where ultimately there is no exit except out, unless checked and addressed in a firm and positive manner.

"Persona" is a controllable state and I will devote a chapter in this book to the whole issue of changing your "persona" in a positive/warm way. I think that you will be well pleased with the end results if you apply some of the thoughts in there.

There was a phrase I remember at school which very aptly describes it all for me.

It goes as follows: It is not who wins or loses the game of life that matters; it is how you play the game that counts!

This not only applies to the integrity and charitable person that you should aspire to live your life with. I think it also applies to the person that your "persona" should aspire to warm towards or the color that you should aspire to glow to.

You owe it to yourself to be the best that you can be and there are no short cuts in between, period! I think that the inner soul of this book is really all about that!

Roy Taylor

Chapter 6

What About Me And My "Persona"?

Let's take a moment and breathe in and out a few times, relax and try to absorb what we have addressed so far. In order for us to look at ourselves, we need to think hard about what we have covered so far. Do you have a strong grasp on what a cool/blue/negative "persona is and what a warm/orangey, red/positive "persona" is? If you are ready to look at yourself, then I must very strongly suggest that you need to be fiercely honest and hard on yourself to attempt this extremely important step. Are you ready? Good! Then let's begin.

First of all I am going to surprise you a little and suggest that we are not going to break down our whole being in any normal fashion; what we are going to do is to get a piece of regular-lined letter pad and we are going to draw two vertical lines top to bottom down the sheet at equal intervals dividing the page into three equal parts.

In the first part of the page we will put a heading "Bottom Drawer." In the second part of the page we are going to make a heading that says "Middle Drawer," and in the third section on the right side of the page we should put a heading "My Dream Persona."

The Bottom Drawer

In the "Bottom Drawer" this is the most important part of the process. I want you to in number order down the page on each line as many as you need to write, to list everything in your previous life from today, that was bad to the extent that it had a bad effect on you and it still bothers you and put it in the "Bottom Drawer". It is really important to take as long as you need on this section, one day, one week, whatever it takes to get them all in this list. To give you a few examples, how about molestation, neglect, abuse, physical abuse, rape, bad childhood events, if you think of them, they count o.k. you don't make a call on them yourself. How about bad grades at school, failures, broken home, broken marriage, had a child adopted and regret it, never had a child and wanted one, bad relationship with a family member, anything that you consider has or had a negative influence in your life. Now the rule is simple, you can open this drawer anytime and put another item on the list o.k.? Once the list is full to the extent that you feel you are ready to move on, I want you to read all the items on the list and consider that this is the last time that you are going to worry or think about them again, you must make a commitment to forgive any personalities that may exist in the list as a result of what part they played in making the item a part of the list, I did not say that you are going to make friends with them again I simply said to forgive them. How do I forgive?

There are several ways, but the best way I know is to vision that person as needing a whole lot of help, because a good person wouldn't be like that and then make a pact with yourself that you will not think of them with any anger again and shut them out of your life emotionally. If you can forgive them and you feel alright to keep them in your life, you need to understand that if they stay in your life, that the incident or events that have caused you to put them in your "Bottom Drawer" must be completely buried and removed from your future life with them, if you think you can do it, then more power to you that is great, if you are on the fence on this, you should consider first of all what it is that makes you feel that way towards them. Could you be a part of the problem? If you feel that you may be a contributor to the problem then first of all you might need to put these people on the back burner while you work on your own "persona", certainly you owe it to you and them to have a very frank conversation about what you are feeling towards them and ask them how they feel. If you decide after taking this course of action that the relationship has a chance of recovery, then put it on hold if you decide that there is no chance of recovery then make the physical break with them and start life afresh there are no alternatives if you cannot rid your mind of the pain they have caused.

You see, the "Bottom Drawer" is a place that we will only go back to add to and that will be on a new sheet of paper when we do. We will not read any of the items on the list again; they will be wiped from our mind in the best way possible for every day living and when they try to raise their miserable heads we will gently move on to some other subject in our mind or even create one and try to keep them in the "Bottom Drawer," something to help you feel better on how to do this when you think about them; imagine closing a very large drawer in your mind and then think of something really nice, a tropical island scene or a huge ice cream cone with nuts and topping, whatever makes you feel good.

The whole issue here is to approach your whole life in a positive and pleasant way, by the way praying works for lots of people and I highly recommend it if you have a faith where you find comfort in your everyday life. The key though, is to get rid of the bad things that you have carried with you in life. It is not unlike carrying a 100 pound sack of rocks on your back up a steep hill , obviously we don't want to take them all the way back down the hill to get rid of them, so we will lay them down right here (put them in the "Bottom Drawer") and carry on with our life (up the hill). I hope that pictorial image sticks with you, because it really is a good analogy of what may well be going on in your life right now and we need to free your soul and spirit for the exciting things that lie ahead without all these burdens to haul with us.

Now we need to cut the "Bottom Drawer" list off the sheet with a pair of scissors vertically at the dividing line to the next section and then we need to place it in a dark place in a closet or old shoe box or a safe and as we place it wherever we are going to place it, we need to say to ourselves, "that's it, what's past is past" and then close your mind to what is in there forever, with forgiveness and good thoughts to replace them. This is a tough challenge, but you can do it and if you don't think you can, then don't leave this place until you find a way to do it, talk to a professional or a clergyman or someone you trust, tell them what you are trying to do and ask for their help. Please take the time to deal with this list properly; you cannot move on until you have it under your control to such an extent that it will not be in your life from today onwards.

Easier said than done you might say, yes that is true but nevertheless it is the only solution that I can think of. Too many people live their lives blaming the rotten life they are living on their past. We cannot live a full and happy life if we dwell on negative stuff all the time and then use it as a crutch to explain why they are such a cool/blue/negative "persona" they may not call it a "persona" but that is the aura they give off and it impacts everyone around them in some way, so be fully aware of how destructive the past can be. It can consume every thing in one's life and sometimes we don't even know it.

"The Bottom Drawer" is a place in your soul that has a bad tenant and it needs to be evicted in a forceful persuasive manner, so that is why I want you to cut it off the page of GOOD things.

Let's pursue the eviction of the "Bottom Drawer" a little further. If you are not really sure of what it is that is causing you to feel blue or cool, then take a little private time and do something you really enjoy doing, something that you may not have done for years; apply yourself to it earnestly with all the enthusiasm you can find and do it often and repeatedly for a while, maybe forever if that makes you feel good. Do it and somewhere during the time frame after a week or couple of weeks. Take a look at how it has made you feel being absorbed in something wholesome and good, even if you resort back to the bad thoughts in between. Take a look at how you feel when you are doing this special activity. It can be a sport, a hobby, reading, driving, riding, you name it, whatever makes you happy. This is the feeling I want you to capture in your life and I want you to use it to find out what makes you feel bad and also now to realize what makes you feel good.

If you can bring these feelings forward in your mind, then you now will be able to work on expunging the bad things on to the "Bottom Drawer" list. Remember what I said before, and when you discover what is making you feel low or blue inside can be added to the "Bottom Drawer" any time and it can be on a sticky note or a little scratch sheet and it is then put in the dark place with the original list. The bad stuff must be put away and put in a dark place.

Let's address a couple of issues that I think are side-effects of the pain caused by "Bottom Drawer" items and a seriously major cooling influence on our society as a whole: alcoholism and drug abuse. Both of these aggressive side effects are huge indicators of a blue or cool/negative "persona" and to be honest they develop in a person's life for many reasons: tough home life, bad parental relationship, peer pressure, low self-esteem, puberty, genetics. I put genetics at the end of a list that can go on forever. Let me say this: I think that almost all of the reasons are excuses. They are a cop out from life and can be controlled if the individuals themselves can just find the inner self-control and strength to address their problems head on and make a strong attempt to change their "persona." In other words, I think that we have the power to control our "persona" and failure to do so results in the quality of life that we live, period! You might be thinking, that is a high and mighty opinion for someone who isn't an alcoholic, yes you may be right, but I can honestly say that in my own life, I have gone through a period when on a night out with fellow peers, I would drink fourteen to sixteen pints of beer and finish the evening on a half a bottle of scotch, and for a time it was continuous on every occasion possible as a young adult. Was I addicted? Maybe. What made me change? I am sure that almost everyone goes through a period in the growth of a habit where they know what they are doing is wrong and harmful to their body and the decision time for continuing is existent, succumbing to the temptation is very appealing; the solution is this: recognize the issue, drinking, smoking, drugs, whatever and make a 180 degree turn in your every day routine. Do nothing that resembles the lifestyle that you have been living and take it one day at a time reinforcing the success of each day with a daily reward for success and on days of failure no reward and a mental check on the reasons for the change in lifestyle. Too often everyday pressures cause the problem and they all need to be placed in the "Bottom Drawer".

What about work, bringing up kids, paying everyday bills? Well there are more ways than one to work, different kinds of work are a choice. Kids can be taken into different environments that make them easier to enjoy or they can be brought into check if they are out of hand. Paying bills involves either finding more pay for the hours worked or more hours of work which can be handled individually or jointly with a partner; the point is, nothing is very often as big as it seems close up and we tend to magnify our problems out of all proportion and that can certainly affect our "persona." Rest assured though, my solutions are tough sometimes but that is what it takes to be in control of our lives. The tougher our lives the tougher and more observant of ourselves we need to be!

Once we have identified the painful things that cause us to hurt, we need to make a pact that we are ready to move on in our lives and that is when we move on to the second column on our sheet which is headed by the title "Middle Drawer".

The Middle Drawer

The "Middle Drawer" is where we need to look at all the great things that exist in our lives, NOTE! Even the toughest lives have good things going on in them, again spend lots of time writing the list as long as you can, this can be , relationship with spouse, kids, work, play, camping, cooking, sport, home, car, everything you can think of. Build the list big and LONG o.k. and keep adding to it as you live your life. These are the important things in your life and you need to take a good hard look at whether this list is better for you than the one you have evicted to a dark place.

These are the things that keep us sane and these are the positive/warm/orangey/red influences in our life that take our "persona" color from dark blue/ cold/ negative to the color that you are today, whatever it is. Keep in mind that the color your "persona" is really the balance of weight that the two lists exert on your "persona". If you are a light bluish "persona", then your "Bottom Drawer" is out weighing your "Middle Drawer". Does that make sense? I hope so, because life is nothing but balance and if you want a good life with a warm "persona", then you need to reinforce and grow the list in the "Middle Drawer" it is that simple, in my opinion, nothing more nothing less.

Well we now have a "Middle Drawer" so what, again, I would like you to cut it off vertically on the line between that and the next column with a pair of scissors and I would like you to put it on display in your home, on the fridge, in the office, in the toilet, over the bath, somewhere that doesn't upset your spouse, maybe on a small clip board and read it every day first thing in the morning before you start your day. In addition to that I want you to put a calendar on the wall near it showing the month at a glance and I want you to make a goal to put on that calendar every day, an event that you want to achieve that day that is either in the :Middle Drawer" or that could be added to the "Middle Drawer" if it goes on the calendar then it must be worthy of the "Middle Drawer and it must be added to the "Middle Drawer if it goes on the calendar, first and foremost, it must be pleasurable to you.

Let's say you like playing with the kids at the park, then do it and put it on the calendar to do at a specific time. If you love playing chess, then make a date with someone to play that day. Make it practical around your daily calendar. Here is a very important NOTE, ever heard the phrase "bored people are boring" yes it is true, the other phrase "idle hands make the devil's work" yes that is true also. How about asking someone to do something at night and they complain that they are tired, well that is nonsense! You are never too tired to live a good life and life should be lived until you go to bed o.k. Got It? Good! So from now on, tired people are boring and you are not one of them ever again. Why am I being so tough on these guys, well people do get tired, we all get tired but we should never be that tired that we cannot have a good time with family or a friend and when we do cry tired, it is because we want to be boring and that is allowing our blue side to take control o.k.? How about the "idle hands make the devil's work" thought? I believe that this statement is about as true as it gets when you look at youth and idle people, so if you are idle watch it o.k. Youth has a very small loophole as far as I am concerned, it lies with their parents to keep them occupied period! As far as idle adults are concerned, most of them are failures in life, they have blue/ cool/negative "personas" and they need to get a life. It is that simple, if the program I am suggesting is implemented as soon as possible, their life will change. Ok if you are not a disciplined person who will read the list every day and make a calendar booking everyday to do something good then you need a helper, this can be a spouse a partner, a family member, a friend or someone you trust and feel good with who will remind you to do this deed daily and encourage you to maintain the program, whatever it takes to make it happen o.k.?

Let's use an example here. If you are lonely in your life for some reason, then your calendar entry must involve an activity that involves someone else, a friend a club meeting, a sporting event where you can interact with people and so on using the emphasis on being happier and busier and more fulfilled in your life than you feel right now, initially it may not be a pleasurable thing to do, but your positive side must have faith that this is right and good for you in the big picture and you must take the step forward, just like learning to walk, initially it is difficult but after a while it is easy and natural to do it.

The goal is to focus on the good things going on in your life and to prioritize them as the way you want to live your life, at the same time making you feel pleasure and warmth from doing them more often in your life. If it happens to be a spouse that is on your list, then make more fun dates with them, I hope you get the message that it is not the bad things in life that makes us steam along like a well oiled engine, it is the good things and the more often we change the oil the better we run, so make sure that calendar is so full of good stuff that we just don't have time to think of anything else. A word of warning on this subject, make sure that you maintain diversity in your calendar of events, remember you really can have too much of a good thing and that can turn from a warm influence to a cool one really quick. If it does, don't put it in the "Bottom Drawer" just rest it for a while and go back to it later..

The whole point of this method of self improvement is to help you to increase the good activity in your life, to mentally stop thinking about the bad stuff that can make you inactive and to learn to control your emotions by the way you live your life as a whole and once these things start to kick into your every day life style, you will feel like a better person in so many more ways than one. Other people will react to you differently, you will enjoy being present in other people's company more and you will most importantly enjoy your own company more than ever.

If you maintain this program forever it is fine, you may find that after months or years of doing it that you will not need the support as much and you may find that you can handle your life better as a whole and can then continue on your own steam, however you never want to stop self analyzing your way of living life and put checks into place that you need to refresh in certain places. I think that if you find that you are slipping in any way that you should certainly get back on the "Middle Drawer" program as soon as possible, so don't drop it too quick or even at all. You are never too old to make this happen.

Dream "Persona"

The moment is here that I absolutely LOVE the best; this is the place where you get to choose what your "Dream Persona" should be. Keep in mind that this is a very powerful mode to be in and you have to treat the decision with extreme caution, it involves not only how you wish to perceive yourself, but also how you wish other people to perceive you. This is awesome power at your fingertips and only you can implement the full effect of this power on yourself. So be careful what you wish for it may come true.

You know how fat people (I am one by the way) perceive themselves, as fat. You know how thin people perceive themselves? As not fat! Yes beauty is in the eyes of the beholder and the way we perceive ourselves emotionally or in our "persona" is strictly the way we allow ourselves to be. Having said that, I want to take you now into a realm that you may not have considered before and that is the spectrum of control of our spirit our being and our physical make up. The truth is that we all have the power to change anything we like or don't like about ourselves and unfortunately we also have the power to accept what we are and not exert any energy into that change. I hope that by reading this book so far that I have given you a little of what I feel about my fellow humans and also a little bit more about looking at oneself in a more aware way to become more observant about the factors that influence our inner being. The key is that we are aware; it does not matter whether we agree or disagree with the observations and correction strategies suggested in this book, but to be aware means we know better and should address our lives and our relationships accordingly.

If we have the power to control our very being, then why don't we all do it? A very tough question, but an important one we all need to ask ourselves. Primarily, I think most people lack self-confidence in their own ability to make changes to their own "persona;" many have no idea what it is all about and others just don't care and think that everyone else can take them or leave them just the way they are.

The bottom line however, is that if presented in just the right way, I believe almost everyone would choose to be a much better "persona" than they presently are, if only they could bury the past and the bad things that have influenced their growth in life to the "persona" that they currently are.

With those thoughts in mind, it is time to take the challenge!

When I first thought about writing this book, I thought to myself, what is a "Dream Persona" I came up with several thoughts on this subject, but hit a wall in several areas. The problem is that we are all different, even if we were brought up identical and lived an identical life, we would still have different "persona" characteristics and consequently we would all have varying degrees of warm and cool in our "persona." That is what is so complex about this subject and what I find so fascinating about it.

My conclusion was that there must be many different "Dream Personas." What is for one may be completely different to another and that is great, because it adds spice to our lives, good for some and not for others and that is fine, we need to accept and understand that always.

In planning what your "Dream Persona" should look like, you need to now go to the remaining column on your now cut up page and put down on that list all the things that you consider to be right and good about all the people you know or admire. These are personality characteristics, looks, beliefs, demeanor, warmness, LOVE and ways of showing it, success in business, success in life, charitability, religious commitment, sporting prowess and any and all things that you can think of that you would aspire to have and then try to feel what each item on your list would feel like if you had that in your "persona," then take a look at yourself deeply and decide if you already have that particular asset in your being.

Top Drawer

Here it comes! Get out that letter size note pad and tear off one more sheet of paper, at the top of the whole page write in BIG BOLD writing "Top Drawer." Yes we need a "Top Drawer" this is where we need to go every day of our life and it needs to be the intimate details of how we are going to get there.

First of all below the title "Top Drawer," draw a line vertically down the middle of the page. On the top left column of the page we need to write all the things that we find in our "Dream Persona" list that we believe that we already have. Make the list as long as you can based upon your observations from the "Dream Persona" list; you can be gentle and forgiving with yourself in creating the list. If there is even a glimmer in your personality that you may have a quality like that, then add it to the list.

Next on the same page at the top right side I want you to write the things that you don't think you have right now but believe you can achieve with effort and commitment. Isn't it amazing how being slim goes right to the top of that column?. Yes, great minds think alike!

As you build the two columns, it may become apparent that you may have more in the left column than the right; to me, that indicates that you have some esteem and that you have hope in your own mind that you can improve on what you already have. If you have more on the right hand list than the left, then we have some work to do. You may not be being fair with yourself and there may be items on your right hand list that should be on your left hand if you just gave yourself a break and not be so hard on yourself. Alternatively you may just be short on the "Dream Persona" list and you need to spend more time on it. Remember the "Dream Persona" needs to be the all encompassing idea that you have of a perfect "persona:" warm, glowing when you enter a room, people just love to be around you for all kinds of good reasons, you possess conviction to your beliefs, you have a deep faith in your fellow mankind, you are honest, good-looking maybe? You are happy with your lot, being alone with yourself, accepting the faults of the people who surround you without judgement,you show tranquility in your disposition and you smile a lot, being around you just feels good.

Get what I mean? Good. Don't mistake having wealth or fame as having a great "persona;" some people clutch at wealthy or famous people because some of it may rub off and the wealthy or famous ones get a false sense of comfort from this state of being thinking that everyone LOVES them when in fact it may be quite to the contrary; if they weren't wealthy or famous which means they had nothing in the first place and need to work really hard on their own "persona".

These steps that I have outlined should each be taken on as a major project in your life and should be given the importance that they represent in the improvement of your life and if possible should be kept to yourself with the exception of the "Middle Drawer" project until you have completed all phases of the program to your own satisfaction, that way you will be able to monitor the success of it in your own perception of your life and other people's perception of you.

As you build the lists in the "Top Drawer" you need to also consider what you need to do in your life to better improve the qualities you possess in the left hand column and also what you need to initiate in your life to bring the right hand column into play in your life all these qualities are things that somewhere in your mind, you have decided that they are sufficiently important that they would be things and characteristics that you would aspire to have or be in your "persona", that being the case, it is very important that we prioritize these lists as a future project on ourselves beginning today! Remember that we need to start something in order to finish it, well we may never finish this project but we sure as eggs are eggs (forgive my English colloquialisms) are going to give it our best try at success RIGHT?

In order to decide how to go about improving our qualities on the left column, the ones we believe that we might possess already in even the smallest dosage, is to take each item by item and make a paragraph or two on a separate sheet of paper on each item about the individual qualities you like about that particular item and what you feel that you are not doing in order to enhance that particular feature in your "persona". For example, let's say that an item on that list is "Patience", you don't have much but you do have a little. First of all, we need to look at what patience is, it is staying cool in ones self when things don't happen as fast as we would wish, It is not allowing ourselves to get agitated when things take longer than anticipated. It is having the ability to stay at a particular task much longer than you want to. The dictionary says the following:

Patience   handling pains or trials calmly or without complaint.

Manifesting forbearance under provocation or strain.

Not hasty or impetuous.

Now we know what the true meaning of the word is, we need to recall this explanation at all times when we feel the urge to be impatient. Yes it is that simple and that difficult. We need to learn self discipline in this area as a method of improving our skill here.

To be quite honest, once you start to take a truly analytical approach to the positive traits in a "persona" that you feel would make you a warmer, better "persona" the rest will slowly fall into place, if you truly want to achieve the improvements that you have listed.

If you have a list of items in the right hand column and you would truly like to possess those qualities in your "persona' then you need to look at the real reason why you don't feel that you have that particular quality and then determine if it is realistic for you to develop it. Maybe, it is not an attainable characteristic. For example, you may not see yourself as beautiful to other people. The truth is, beauty is in the eyes of the beholder and you probably are far more beautiful than you think no matter what you do to yourself you will not become more beautiful than you already are, maybe manicuring your hair or using make-up a little more pleasingly would help you to feel better or if you are a man then perhaps dressing a little more caringly or simply making a commitment to not think about it in a judgmental way anymore and that also goes for how you look at others also. This really should not be in this column it should be in the left column, you just may not be as objective about it as you need to be, maybe you haven't met the right person yet, and maybe you aren't going out enough to meet the right person. Maybe you need to work on all the other things on the lists, as you do, your beauty will grow and grow. So don't be hard on yourself. Oh! Yes, while I am on the subject of being hard on you, people with a low self esteem can be very hard on themselves and this is the place where we move on from that kind of thinking pattern. We no longer dwell on the bad things and we act from now on like we don't have anything we are ashamed of physically or mentally, it is a downer on your "persona" and it needs to be in the "Bottom Drawer" be proud of who you are physically and don't get bent out of shape trying to improve things it is just a statement your mind is making that says you feel insignificant and are self conscious o.k. Move On! I have a great analogy for this, Remember going into a crowded room full of people who mostly know each other except they don't know you? You get all wound up feeling very self conscious and you walk in the room and yes your right, you know no one so you walk up to the first smiling face and say hello, ever wondered why it is the one that is smiling? Because they appear to be "WARM". Moving on with my thought, after a while that person introduces you to someone else and soon you are making lots of new friends and you feel good. That is exactly what I am saying about beauty, it is skin deep and people are beautiful in so many ways and once they make friends with themselves things feel good inside, not self conscious and squeamish any more about being around other people or themselves.

The "Middle Drawer" attributes that you perceive to be existent inside your "persona" already, need to be individually nurtured and cultivated daily and practiced and improved until perfected. Once these are in place as a solid job in progress list, we need to monitor their success on a weekly basis, just take a few minutes maybe on a weekend day and look at your check list which you need to jot down in a note pad when a breach in the plan occurs during the week and identify why you failed in the objective to handle that event or situation differently than you did. Don't make it hard work on yourself, but be objective and if you feel you can handle it internally in your mind then do so it will be far more successful if you can and are able to correct it as you go along, the most important thing is that you notice when you don't do it right and reward yourself mentally when you do. Being able to deal with everyday life situations in your mind, means that you are truly learning the art of self-control and that is the gift that we all need to obtain a "Dream Persona. A place where we have complete control of our being and our "persona" with the knowledge that others may only enter with our permission and others may not have the ability to manipulate our "persona" the way they want it to be. That is truly being in a place that we choose to be.

Only when we are at this level of control of our spirit do we have permission to be the "persona" that we choose to be, dare I say it, either warm or cool: you choose!

I have learned from experience that the greater part of our happiness or misery depends on our dispositions and not on our circumstances.

Martha Washington

Chapter 7

Can I Change My "Persona?"

So far in this book I have covered the issues that I believe help to mold our "persona" and I also hope that the previous chapters have helped to create awareness that there is more going on within us and our fellow mankind than the surface appearance that everyone conveys in their everyday demeanor. That inner glow that we all possess has an enormous impact on our relationships and our successes and failures in life, and if properly addressed the glow can be warmed to a higher level if there is a true determination to make a positive change.

In order to raise the level of warmth we have in our "persona" there are some basic rules to follow and they are really quite simple as long as we keep them in a priority position in our thoughts about how we go about our everyday behavior and lifestyle, things will start to change. For some it will be quicker and easier than for others. A little like a fitness program; if one doesn't keep working at it, the body deteriorates into an unfit mode. If an individual wants to warm or make his "persona" warmer, he needs to keep at the remedy on a consistent and regular basis, unlike the fitness program, it is an ongoing change of one's complete way of dealing with people and life's challenges every hour of the day.

So where do we go from here? First of all I think it would be smart to break the program down into stages and to tackle the changes at different levels of intensity, so that they can be more easily achieved. I thought about this a lot with the goal of making it a believable, nourishing experience for all who tried the program. After all if no good things happen fairly quickly, the transformation may not be followed through to its positive orangey/red conclusion and that would concern me a great deal. I want this to be incredibly successful and for all those who commit to the change to enjoy a whole new enriched life full of wonderful experiences and for those with relationships that are less than dream-like, to experience improvement in those relationships or at least, find a way to have peace themselves in their own life regardless.

Let's get started: the first part of our adventure should be in addressing our own physical demeanor. The things that we look for in other people, I don't mean specifically clothing or make-up or manicuring, but I am including them to some degree, so let's get them out of the way right away.

As far as appearances are concerned, and this may not apply to many, but for those that this does apply to please be realistic and accept true responsibility. If you are in the habit of not following personal hygiene disciplines rigorously then this is step one. Make changes immediately; freshen up with a hot shower daily and comb hair, use a nice deodorant and a little cologne or mild perfume (not the sickly kind). I think stay at home spouses can fall into the rut of looking like they have been dragged through a hedge backwards and expect their nearest and dearest to accept them just the way they are. Is this positive? NO! If you are a guy and you do a hard manual job every day and dirt is as much a part of your life as eating and drinking, it is not sufficient to come home, complain about your day and kick back on the couch in front of the TV. The change needs to be as follows: come home, have a shower, put on fresh clothes or nightwear and eat dinner with the wife and kids if there are any. If it is too late for the kids then make sure that they get a good night kiss and hug at least. Anyway the point is we do not need to dress up but we also do not need to look like something the dog dragged in either! Remember, cleanliness is next to Godliness and who can argue with that? The purpose of this part of our program is to achieve two things: first, when we are freshened up and tidy, it makes us feel good, secondly, when we are freshened up we freshen our minds also, the very act of washing and combing our hair is mentally stimulating and it shows to those around us that we care about ourselves and we have self-esteem.

Please note, I am not insinuating everybody has bad personal hygiene, but I am suggesting that some let things slip when they are confined to the home or are in a career choice that doesn't demand high standards or if life is at a low point and depression is getting the better of one. There is no need to carry those standards any further than necessary and at the earliest opportunity; it is good to refresh one's mind and spirit in a physical way. Today's fashion of having vibrant color streaks in the hair and pants that hang off the butt with chains attached is not positive in fact it is quite the opposite, the majority of normal people are uncomfortable around these statements of dress and presentation and will react to it with a negative response, I am not suggesting that all modern trends are negative, but I am suggesting that ghoulish presentations are not warm and never will be, included in that are nose rings and tongue studs no matter what the claim of enhanced libido are, it just isn't pleasant and warm to see or be around.

While on this subject, I am convinced that there is a very large group of our youth in today's society who are suffering greatly as a result of many things, but in my opinion it is primarily neglect, yes neglect, I think these kids that dress up like ghouls and listen to filth are lacking in parental control and that interprets into lack of displays of LOVE and an interest in who they are and what they are by their parents and their reaction to this situation is rebellion against society and a dress code that challenges their parents to do something about it the worse the better it appears so if you are a parent of one of these rebels, make a stand and ban it from their choices, period and that goes for their friends also, ban yours from mixing with them. Be strong on this, if you once start, follow it through to conclusion, no matter how tough the resistance is o.k.?

Moving on, once the issue of basic appearance at home and outside the home is in control, the next step is very important, smile a lot more, try not to frown and when looking at close ones or strangers, smile a warm and friendly smile and do it often, that alone will make people react a lot differently, most people think they are already warm and don't need to do much as they already smile, not true, almost nobody smiles enough, that is the simplest and easiest thing to practice, it makes a huge difference to everyone around, just do it, it is fun and it works. The habit of smiling a lot will make many things change and it will put a whole new slant on the way people see you it may even help some to see life a little differently in a happier sort of way.

Another very simple but important change to consider, is the way one walks and also the way one sits down, strange? Not really, have you ever watched a person who walks into a room with their shoulders scrunched and they don't look straight in front of them but look down to the ground they avoid eye contact with others as though they are ashamed of themselves or that they don't want to have to strike up a conversation with you. These are negative characteristics and my suggestion to handle this if you are that kind of person is to straighten your posture look ahead of you and make eye contact with everyone and everyone whilst smiling at the same time. It demonstrates that you are proud and that you care about the people and things around you, people will react positively to this (remember, don't forget to smile!).

I mentioned sitting, yes sitting down is a statement also. If a person slouches at the dining table or just relaxing, it can be interpreted as a message that you are lazy, disinterested in the surrounding company or that you are bored, remember bored people are boring, DO NOT give off that aura it is negative and it won't make your life or "persona" any better. Look the world in the eye like you are someone special and walk and sit like you are someone to be respected, it works, believe me.

Here are a few other thoughts while on the subject of appearance and how others perceive us, if you are with family, always try to say nice things, If you have an urge to be harsh or plain nasty, stop, don't say it, instead say something nice or don't say anything at all, the family will respond positively to this behavior and in time it will prove to be a very positive action.

Compliment often and meaningfully, it is appreciated by everyone whether they say it or not and will definitely make your day a little better overall for doing it, which will make you a little warmer also. Try to think about what you want to say before saying it, for those that run at the mouth, can emit a strong negative aura without really knowing it. Sometimes the result of talking without thinking can be offensive to others and statements made without tact can be hurtful and often cannot be retracted once they have been made. If you suffer with this problem, the best thing to do is not to talk when the others are talking and make brief significant statements, don't ramble on it is boring and you know about that already RIGHT?

Don't use foul language if you are a guy and especially if you are a gal, it offends many more than it pleases and for those friends it doesn't offend, maybe a fresh choice of friends is in order! There is no room for vulgarity in any situation; it is a statement of weakness of character in those that use it as a crutch. If effort is made on any or all of the issues that apply above, immediate results should be noticed and this plan should be followed forever. Just be strong enough to accept the weaknesses you possess if you have them and start the changes right away with yourself and your LOVED ones and friends and co-workers, in fact everyone.

Let's move on to step number three, which I think is a hard one to grasp especially if you are used to living life in the fast lane and haven't really stopped long enough to breathe. Never mind do this!

Make personal time for yourself everyday. Personal time can be used in many ways, but one must always keep the true objective in mind and that is to find a place of peace and tranquility where one can reflect on the good things around and the good relationships that one has and the friends or family members who need your attention for whatever reasons. One might initially think that it is impossible to make that kind of time on a daily basis, not so, if you take a look at your day no matter how busy you are, there are many times in the day when you can ponder your true inner thoughts and I will make a few suggestions on how to plan it into your schedule. Obviously everyone has a different schedule but there are certain times that most of us share in common; first of all take a look at what you do when you get up, do you have a cup of tea or coffee if so what do you usually do while you drink that drink, can the time be modified to personal time? How about the drive to and from work, can the radio be turned off and the time used to better purpose, Lunch time, is all of it fully used up with co-workers socializing, try halving that time with them and applying the remainder to your own time. At night, is TV so important you can't apply twenty or thirty minutes to yourself, what about when you are walking the dog? So many opportunities, the truth is we often just don't apply ourselves to the important things and this time is extremely meaningful, it is a time when we indulge ourselves with our own thoughts and feelings. We must ensure that the time is used for good thoughts though, if we apply the time to angry or bad thoughts, it will serve no purpose at all, other than to make our "persona" cooler and darker. The real purpose is to help ones mind to take a revitalizing break and to recharge it with positive impulses which will help to make the project of warming one's "Persona" a little easier to achieve. The time we spend on this process can be as long as we like as long as we don't turn it into lethargy, and we must consciously make an effort to do it every day, it doesn't have to be the same time or the same event, but it does need to take place!

For many years I demonstrated the true symptoms of a work-a-holic but it never made me feel down or depressed there were two main reasons I attribute to that, and that was first of all the support I got from my wife who always handled the long hours positively, and because we both realized it was a necessity in order to survive and secondly, I used my car time for my own sanity, I would think about all the nice things I wanted for us as a family and for myself once I had made my fortune successfully in the business world. I would ponder my individual family members and my friends and I always felt that was good valuable time spent that didn't intrude in my working everyday life.

There is a golden rule however; the cell phone gets switched off during this time!

Here is another way to make some private time, if you don't already have one, take up a meaningful hobby, this is so valuable a way to use

your time, it is rewarding and educational and positive in so many ways
and it gives you programmed private time without any effort if you
choose the right hobby.

Step number four involves using some more of your time to positive
ends, it requires a truly deep commitment to the cause and cure and
it requires unselfish behavior to truly achieve success, but the rewards
are enormous beyond all expectations. Wow! What can this miraculous
event be we ask?

The answer lies in doing something for someone else, that's it? Yes
that's it, plain and simple. What kind of thing you might ask? First of
all you need to pick a truly charitable meaningful thing to do at least
once a month, preferably every week. It must be charitable in nature
preferably not monetary, in other words you need to give of yourself
and someone else less fortunate needs to benefit from your actions.
For those who are now questioning my program, I challenge you to ask
yourself if you have ever in your life done an act of this nature and if you
have not, give me the benefit of the doubt and try it. If you have done
something in your lifetime and not for many years and just didn't get a
kick out of it, I challenge you to ask yourself if your "persona" is really
much darker blue than you care to admit, no matter what, you must
make the effort. The purpose is multifold, but primarily it is a totally
unselfish activity that is driven by good warm thoughts and I think you
will find the benefits so powerful an influence to your "persona" that
you will want to do more and more and people will perceive you in a
whole new light, especially if you smile a lot while you talk about it to
others and smile a lot when you perform the activity.

Some years ago I was very heavily involved in the Rotary
International organization which is a worldwide group of businessmen
who meet every week at a prescribed location for breakfast, lunch or
dinner depending on the individual club and at these meetings the
purpose was for businessmen to get to know each other in all different
fields of business which was beneficial if one needed a plumber or an
accountant or travel agent etc. The other more powerful reason was
the charity work performed by this group on a Local and National
and International level the involvement was anything from a charity
Golf tournament to visiting a local hospital and talking with very sick
people to fund raising to help eradicate polio on an International level.
I remember playing Santa Clause for many years to children from the
poorest families in the neighborhood, literally thousands of kids over
the years and I tell you, I loved that role and each and every child that
sat on my lap that believed in Santa Clause made the experience all

the more rewarding, it cannot be replaced, so my challenge to you, is to find a niche where you can make a meaningful impression on your fellow man and pursue it. I should say that there are many wonderful organizations in addition to Rotary International and they include Lyons Clubs, Kiwanis and a host of others the list is longer than my arm and they can be found in any community, almost anywhere around the world.

Step five involves a serious lifestyle commitment, one which I have avoided my whole life, but one I have only committed seriously to this year. This one is tough for some and not so for others, but the need is great metabolically and physically for all of us and I truly believe that it makes a big difference in our self perception and that is, working out in a fitness program on a regular basis with consistency and commitment. It isn't necessary to go crazy, but it is necessary to make some resolution to do some exercise even if it is as simple as walking every day. Whatever the choice, stay with it, I know it is tough and I know it takes effort to stay with it but for those of you who battle with that one, relax in the thought that I am going through it with you, so far so good and I plan to stay with it! please note I am not talking about weight here, I am merely talking about doing some exercise with the sole purpose of making ones body feel energized, if weight loss follows for those that need it, then so be it. A suggestion on this one, ask a family member or friend to do it with you, that way you can encourage each other to keep doing it and ultimately it will become a habit you will be glad you started.

Step six involves restraint; this is a very tough challenge to those of us who over indulge in so many different ways, it can be overeating, drinking, smoking, junk food, swearing, sex, any over indulgent excesses need to be brought into check and put into the normal person reasonable situation category. The problem with over indulgent behavior is that it is our inner selves allowing us to be weak and selfish or weak and pathetic either way it is not acceptable as a standard of a warm orangey/ red "persona" lack of self discipline is usually where it all starts to go to blue and negative rather fast so beware!

Make yourself a brief mental checklist of things that you feel need attention or things that others have made you aware of and try to control them, if it is difficult initially then take small steps and don't give up o.k.? Untidiness, laziness, chocolate, coffee, it has so many heads that we often don't notice that we over indulge in these things, but most of us are aware that we do certain things that we shouldn't and we still do it. Let me say this, indulgence in such things in excess is a statement that we need to recognize. Usually, it is a statement that we are looking for a crutch for some other thing that is going on in our heads and the only way to take full control of our being is to exercise restraint to the extent that we indulge in these things only when it is normal and acceptable to do so anything more than that is to allow our negative side to be in control and that means our "persona" is affected also by our actions. To be in control is to be strong and to be strong is powerful and that is positive for our "persona". If you find that you have an addiction to something, be aware that that in itself will give you a very negative "persona" and whilst you may not see it in yourself, it probably is quite strongly noticeable to those who know you and live around you. I realize that quitting a habit or addiction can be very difficult, but ultimately it is you who need to take control and that means the strongest of commitments to restraint. Sometimes it is not possible to do it alone and if it means asking for help then do so, keep in mind I said help, you still have to find a way to control it yourself no matter who helps.

I like to tell the story of how I gave up cigarettes it is a testimony for those of you who say easier said than done. I smoked for close to 22 years and I smoked heavily, I was a true addict and I had tried on many occasions to give up without success. The truth is that I had never set my mind that I was going to be in control of those little white coffin nails, every time I gave up, I was thinking about how bad I felt and how badly I needed one and what to do with my hands and always after I had finished that pack. Well I believe I didn't really want to do it bad enough and so any excuse was o.k. to carry on. That is the trouble with addiction, it plays games with your mind and you convince yourself that the pain of giving up is worse than the consequences of carrying on, not so!

The last time I quit about twenty years ago, I had run out of cigarettes at home and I was anxiously rummaging from drawer to drawer trying to find any forgotten packs of cigarettes that may be lying hidden somewhere, to save having to go to the store for more. I found myself lighting a partially smoked butt from an ash tray and was disgusted with myself and made an instant commitment that I would be the controller of this relationship from now on and as of that moment I gave up, The following morning I went to work and on the desk was a pack which contained seventeen cigarettes in it and I decided to leave them right where they lay on the desk as a reminder to myself that I was in control of them, not vice versa. To add to the program, I decided to reward myself for every day that I had succeeded. I put one dollar into a pot on the fireplace each morning. The last time I put a dollar in the pot

I had $162.00 in the pot and decided to go it alone thereafter. I tossed the pack of cigarettes that had so faithfully tried to lure me back every day into the trash and never missed them for a moment. I was proud to have won the battle. It worked; I could still smoke a cigarette today but never will again. I am in control and very much so where they are concerned. Believe me; if I can do that, you can also.

The whole concept of over-indulgence is to initially spoil yourself or to do an act of rebellion or perhaps to get a high of some sort and once we grasp that as the reason for it happening, we can take the steps to control it. If however it passes simple over indulgence and then becomes an addiction, there are multiple reasons to find the strength to battle it. The sooner the better; it can never be a positive addition to anyone's "persona".

Step seven: it's getting more challenging, but if you have addressed each step leading to here, your "persona" is most definitely warmer and more orangey/red than it has ever been and you have no reason to turn back now.

Let's move on. During your life as a participant in family and friendship with others, have you ever felt that you needed more out of your relationships with others? Well in many cases it can be a simple case of changing from a taking relationship to a giving one. The problem with many relationships is that people in them often expect the other party to give to them by way of control, choices, priority, LOVE, emotion, joy, and so many other ways. These expectations are usually destined for some form of misery and usually it is the expector who is going to feel it the worst and the end result is almost always a cooler or bluer "persona;" unfortunately the expectee is going to suffer on this one also. (I hope you liked my two new additions to the English language!). You may well question that it is not always unreasonable to expect the other party to concede some positions and I agree with you; the instances I am referring to are cases of normalcy where a person is just demanding and expects changes or concessions unreasonably. These are cases that cause a lot of aggravation in a household or relationship and again I reiterate that it takes two to tango and so it does also for a relationship to work. Most relationships either work or fail; based upon the amount of selfishness that is present in one or both of the participants it is that simple. The message here is that both parties in a relationship need to give and take unselfishly as much and as often as possible. Warmth is developed by these actions. If it takes just one person to start the cycle then let it be me!

Step eight is a controversial one. It is money. I have always placed money in one place as far as my life is concerned, when I have it I enjoy it and when I don't I work harder to make more. I have to have it to live in our society but I don't have to live for it in any other way and certainly it is not more important than life itself. This philosophy has enabled me to handle some devastating financial losses in my life and I have made and lost two large nest eggs in my life and I have always climbed back. The first time my wife and I lost everything was in a real estate recession and we lost our home and everything else except the clothes on our back.

What survived? Our relationship and our family. Did we starve? NO! It was tough and I learned then that money can be earned again. It is not the driving force in one's life; it is a tool to enable us to have an easier life and a more luxurious life. You noticed I hope that I did not say "BETTER." If money was the way to a better life, all those people in big houses driving big cars would be deliriously happy. I would wager that most of them are quite the opposite if you could sit in their home and listen to what goes on behind the walls of those big homes, I think you might see a lot of stress, pain, unhappiness, ill health, and a host of other problems. I know this does not apply to everyone, some people have control and it is those who truly have control of their "personas" that can enjoy that state without it influencing their "persona." Rest assured though, they are very few and far between.

The problem with money and its influence on people is that for many, they handle it like it was their lifeblood, as though letting go of any will weaken them or destroy them, so they hoard it and live their life fixated on its acquisition, what a miserable way to live! For others, they keep separate accounts within their own household like they don't trust their spouse enough to have equal access to the same account or perhaps they want their own account for selfish reasons so they can indulge themselves secretly without telling their spouses, either way it is selfish and definitely a negative statement to a spousal relationship, that interprets itself as a cooling effect on the "personas" in that relationship.

Money is evil if it is idolized, and it is addictive if it is overindulged as a priority in ones life. I am the first one to say that it is o.k. to make lots of money, what I do say is that it is not o.k. to let the making of it or the ownership of it control your life and the relationships that you have in your life. It is there for the basic necessities of survival and it is there for pleasures, but always in perspective of what it is and always understanding its evil potential!

I think it is important to also address the pursuit of material things whilst on this subject. Money and material things go hand in hand in this context, the pursuit of material things can be as destructive to a "persona" as the pursuit of money, often one thing cannot be attained without the other, if one looks at material things as potentially the sidekick or partner of the other one can easily apply the thoughts I have outlined in this section synonymously one with the other. The real point is that, as long as their pursuit is done with control and it does not take priority over the relationships in one's life and that they are not used as a tool for evil or bad doings, then it is ok to pursue them aggressively, once it is found that relationships are being put in a secondary position on a regular basis, it is time to do a reality check on one's priorities and remember, money and material things can all be earned and bought again so they are not that important in the big picture of life GOT IT? GOOD! Don't forget it!

Step nine is a spiritual challenge, I know that most people who read this book will have some sort of spiritual belief in a GOD or higher being and for those I will challenge you further in this section. However, amongst some of the readers, there will be those who do not have a spiritual belief, I am not qualified to try and convert anyone, but if those who don't really believe in anything will indulge me for a few lines, let's go this direction anyway, I think that it is fundamentally short sighted of anyone who cannot find some kind of belief in a superior being to live their lives and not challenge themselves to explain the incredible world that we live in. It is in my opinion almost inconceivable that the Darwin theory of evolution is plausible. Yes the world has evolved and yes species have developed, but what I cannot buy is any theory that satisfies itself with a big bang or a single celled organism being the basis for life itself. There are too many unexplained issues of where the Universe came from and how any freak of nature could develop an organism as incredibly complicated and different as a human or a dog or a cow or a whale and what about the brain it just cannot be explained, I don't buy the fact that they all came from a single cell and if they did, someone sure gave them a helping nudge to develop into the complexity of a being that you and I are today. Anyway enough of my soap box stuff. My challenge to non believers is that if you give most scriptures, Christian, Buddhism, Muslim etc., there is a basic common ground and that is they all believe in a superior being as the basis for their faith and whether who is right or wrong and whose book is right or wrong is not important, what is important is that they believe in a holy power. The teachings of the Bible, the Curran, the Dalai Lama or whoever also share some common good, they all teach about living a good life and honoring fellow man and the world we live in a nutshell, there is a common good that has formulated the basis for most faiths and whilst some are more extreme than others it is fundamentally good for everyone to at least follow the good beliefs that are the basis of most religions. I know that for some believers these statements may seem contradictory to put one gender of belief alongside another, but the problem with the world today, is that most everyone wants to get the other one to concede that what they believe is better than the other see Step 7. it applies to religion also consequently we have had religious wars throughout history, what none of them seem to grasp is no one knows who really is right or wrong, everyone is entitled to their belief, my problem with non believers is that they don't have a belief in anything and that is a statement that they either don't give a hoot or they just cannot get deep enough within themselves to accept that there are bigger things or beings than them out there. That is a statement of selfishness. Those people are far too concerned with their own importance to accept that they owe their life to a GOD who they cannot see, whose evidence of presence is all around them!

Having upset many of my readers, let's get to the point, the belief in a spiritual presence is a place where humans can go to find peace with their soul, an explanation of their existence and a purpose for their life, that supersedes all else. Miracles do happen, I am a testimony of that and on several occasions in my life I have been the recipient of a miracle and I am a person who would not immediately jump to that conclusion without the event being completely unexplainable. More than luck and more than coincidence and for them I will always be thankful. The point of all this is that when a person finds their spiritual self, they enter a whole new dimension in their life; it is a state of being that enables them to emit an enormously warm aura by way of their "persona" and it also equips them to handle life's challenges in a far more effective and positive way. The preaching's and indoctrination of organized religion can sometimes be unrealistic to the average person, but when combined with a deep spiritual belief, it can enable people to be pleasant to each other, handle the death of a loved one with contentment and sometimes easy acceptance that they are in a better place, it can enable them to participate in acts of unselfish generosity of both time and money, healing by the laying on of hands it can promote better mental attitude and generally create a better and warmer "persona" for even the coolest "personas".

The aspect of deep spiritual belief is so important in a person's life and I must state, if not cultivated by frequent visits to a place of worship, a person's beliefs can be undermined by life's day to day challenges and soon become an insignificant part of their life and then they are exposed to life's challenges without any reinforcement other than what will power they have to face these challenges.

The depth and style of a person's commitment depends on them and that is why I avoided showing any preferences, the point is that it is better to believe in something than nothing at all as long as the foundations are formulated by good wholesome doctrine.

We have covered a lot of thoughts in this chapter and my goal was to break them down individually, I am sure that there are things that you will think of that could enhance the experience of warming your "persona", there are no boundaries on this, as long as they create a warm/positive enhancement to the "persona" then they are o.k. and I say do it if it feels good and it does you good.

If you judge people, you have no time to love them!

Mother Theresa

Chapter 8

A Little Bit About The Author.

I want you to know that I am not a trained psychologist; in fact, I have no medical basis for anything that I write in this book I am a people person. I have spent my whole life dealing and working with people.

I was raised in Africa, in Kenya, and immigrated to England with my parents when I was ten years old, and that was where it all started.

When I arrived in England, I left a dream childhood back in Africa. We had lived within a stone's throw of the whitest beaches in the world; our home was modest, a white-washed single story home that was owned by my grandfather and grandmother, but it had a huge garden which was mainly bush but full of interesting things for a young boy and his friends to explore, including an African village at the end of the fifty acres. It was comprised of five mud huts with palm roofs, where I used to visit when I was on school holiday and the African house keeper's wife or "Bibi" as we called her was meant to baby-sit while my parents went to work. I learned early that the more primitive African people were a happy people with a childish sense of humor who delighted in making jokes about people's misgivings or about sex or about people's ineptitude to perform a physical feat or act and, of course, I was included as a target of their humor on many occasions and enjoyed the camaraderie a great deal. It was simple but warm and friendly, and I remember on many occasions after visiting the village for the day learning how to make a model boat out of a coconut shell or learning how to sniff snuff out of a palm leaf. I know it was naughty but the elders of the village liked me and that was their way of befriending me. I remember the joy that they got when I had a sneezing fit after partaking of that strange stuff.

To go shopping or to go to work or school, we had to drive on a dirt road about five miles to the ferry boat crossing, where we would wait for one of two ferries to arrive every twenty to thirty minutes or so, unload four cars, and then allow us to board for the short trip across Kilindini harbor, which incidentally is one of the deepest natural harbors in the world.

I went to a convent school in those days which was run by the nuns of Loreto, who were very strict about values and behavior. During this time all of my friends, both boys and girls, were the children of other colonials living in the area living a comparatively affluent upbringing.

The life was good; we had wonderful beaches, activities put on by the British Navy boats when they came in to port and held open house on board ship, or when we went inland to Nairobi from our city of Mombasa which entailed a drive of about 360 miles on dirt roads, which when driven would create the most enormous dust clouds. If you were unfortunate enough to be behind someone traveling in the same direction, it was an almost impossible task to see the road in front of you.

It was on those drives that we got to see a wild elephant or rhinoceros or antelope and a host of other game that might have ventured close to the road, or were even standing on the road. Rest assured world reversing-speed records were made when elephants or particularly rhinoceros were stumbled on walking in the road, as they were known to charge and frequently destroys the vehicles that they charged. Such was my early childhood, sheltered yes, but wonderful nevertheless.

When I arrived in England we went to live in a small town called Pevensey Bay in the County of Sussex in Southern England. My life did a one hundred and eighty degree turn. It was my first experience of snow, the worst winter in living memory! I found myself enrolled in a local public school, with a whole different type of child than the ones I was used to.

They were somewhat aggressive in nature, quick to ostracize the stranger from Africa and generally not a pleasant group of children, with bullies amongst them who ran the show on the playgrounds like dictators. I found myself alone and very scared for a while, these guys, boys and girls, didn't like my accent, thought I was stupid because my colonial education lacked the mainstream education of England and had basically put me two years behind my fellow age group. Such is the cruelty of life.

What I think was most noticeable about the English kids in general was that they, through no fault of theirs, seemed to carry a grudge on their shoulder as to why I should have come from a different lifestyle than they and to crown it all spoke differently, even though I was of the same nationality.

Even at ten years old, I remember those nice kids that, regardless of their upbringing, saw their way to help me by offering friendship and kind words of advice on who to watch and what to do, at the specific breaks and changes of class. It was a tough time for me, but this was helped considerably by a few special souls.

I stayed at that school for about eighteen months and left there when my Dad got a job up in the middle of England as a brewer at a famous Midland brewery in Banbury in the County of Oxfordshire.

In Banbury I went back into the public school system and failed the entrance exam for the local grammar school; I had caught up a little on my education but nowhere near enough to pass the national education exam which was developed for 11+ age group and a second chance for late developers at 13+ age group, to determine if you were to go to grammar school and be a leader and white collar worker when you graduated from high school. If you failed, you went to the Secondary Modern School where you were considered to be a potential loser in life and would be destined to a blue collar career and a life of basics. That was the system and I had been cast as a failure through no fault of my own. I remember going to the school for my first day, mixing with the rough and tough kids that were the majority in this educationally segregated sector of the community, and thinking that I was doomed in life and needed to do as well as I could, if I was going to get even a minimal chance in life.

During my tenure at this school I took an interest in the extra-curricular acting class which was held several times a week after school and somehow I got cast in the leading male role as Tutankhamen, in the play Tutankhamen son of Ra. It first played to the whole girls' school and then the whole boys' school, both being on the same campus. I gained enormous notoriety from this and consequently was treated a little like a celebrity around campus, especially with my accent and origin. It helped greatly but I remembered the care free early years and carried an enormous amount of mental anxiety during this time because I felt so different from the other kids around me, who had a different way of thinking and living compared to the life I had grown up with. It was far from fun and my parents, God Bless them, saw it.

My parents decided to send me to a private Preparatory school for boys. Wow, was I in for a learning experience. These were the places where the gentry of England sent their kids to be educated, by rod of iron and strong discipline. My parents were interested in the quality of the education and hoped that this environment would be a help to me in the transition from colonialism to becoming a truly English gentleman!

It started off when I was introduced to the Head Master who was a sadist. He was a man of the Church of England cloth and who delighted in watching the weekly boxing matches which were compulsory for all students to participate in. He also enjoyed the many opportunities he got to administer discipline to the boys for any minor offense like talking to a fellow student in class, or not concentrating on the teacher, in his office.

Here the door was left open for passing students to watch him jump off a stool with a five foot long cane and basically whip them on their bare behinds while the poor student was made to hold the bottom rung of a chair for six repetitions of this punishment, frequently drawing blood with each strike of the cane. Yes I was even more terrified at this school than the previous one, especially when I found out about the students induction ceremony.

It was the custom for the older, senior students to welcome a new boy by taking him first of all in the bathroom and subjecting him to what they called a "bog wash." This meant that he would be forcibly held head first in the toilet bowl which would be previously used and then the toilet was flushed over his head. After that the student was stripped and taken, or should I say carried, outside and thrown naked into the stinging nettle patch. If you have never been stung by a stinging nettle, it is not unlike the feeling you would have if were thrown onto thousands of wasps. Yes it was traumatic, but the reason I am telling you about these interludes in my childhood is because I want you to understand a little about me and how I learned about fellow man and how I tick generally. I feel that it is good to share ones experiences it is what makes us all grow intellectually.

Needless to say I didn't sleep at night very well and I cried a whole lot in the early days of going to that school, but for some inexplicable reason, they didn't get me because they liked me. I was different; and I was from Africa, thank "THE LORD!" Even the bullies got along with me and very quickly, as in the previous school, I found the really nice kids who also extended the hand of friendship to me, which was very timidly accepted.

I didn't, however, escape the boxing matches, which seemed to come around every week awfully fast and I dreaded having to confront my friends in the ring and attempt to beat their brains out: not fun.

I did, however, at this school, stay there a couple of years and during this time, the school got sold and a former headmaster at a reform school took it over. He was a man of extreme discipline also, but he was a fair and just man with a big warm heart, in his sixties, smoked like a trooper and all the boys were treated like his sons. I always remember the day I fell foul of the rules and nearly paid dearly for it.

It was a morning and we were in class awaiting the arrival of our class teacher, when another teacher brought a prospective student's mother on a tour through the classroom and proceeded to move on to the next classroom. Noticing what a good looking woman this was, I let out a wolf whistle to humor my fellow classmates. Unfortunately I was heard by the teacher doing the tour and was called to answer for my actions at the head master's office. I arrived at the door and the door was closed, but there were three little lights to the side of the door; a red one, which move text up meant go away, an orange one, which meant wait, and a green one, which meant come in. My light was orange and eventually after what seemed a decade, the green light came on and I entered his office.

"Taylor," he said, "what is this I have heard about you whistling at one of the mothers?"

I said, "Yes sir, I did, but I was only having fun, sir."

He said, "You know, that is extremely bad manners."

I said, "Yes sir."

He said, "Is there any reason why I shouldn't give you "six of the best?" This meant with a cane on bare behind.

I said, "Yes sir, there is one reason."

He said, "What's that?"

I said, "I have a boil on my backside, sir."

He said, "You do? Show it to me."

I happened at the time to have the biggest boil on my behind and it was angry, so when he saw that I was telling the truth, he gave me detention. Thank "THE LORD."

Well it goes to show that even being a tough disciplinarian, you can have a warm disposition and he certainly was liked by all the students.

I made many friends at that school over the time I was there, but my memory of them is that they were mostly victims of their roots. In other words, their behavior was probably no different than their predecessors and the customs developed within their sphere of growth.

I left that school after about two years and went by my request and my parents sacrifice to the private boarding school my cousin was attending in Guernsey, which is one of those tax-free havens located off the coast of France. In fact, the school I attended, Elizabeth College, had been the German HQ in World War II, where they were planning their invasion of Britain. (Maybe in another book!).

My arrival at this school represented my departure from living at home and a life as a boarder in a school that housed about sixty boarding residents. This was a new experience; here the boys were of affluent upbringing, only this time it included British kids from all over the commonwealth which meant many of them came from similar backgrounds to me. It was a much happier time, even though we slept in dormitories of about thirty boys and the more responsible seniors were given the distinction of being able to administer discipline to any boys found out of line. This included administering the slipper or a referral to the teacher in charge of the boarding house.

I learned what bonding with fellow man was here and how strong relationships can be cultivated in a close-knit community. I also learned how tough unacceptable behavior patterns were treated by the community of residents if people did not behave in a way that befits harmonious living standards. It was a major learning experience for my future life. I learned so many important personality qualities and strengths from going to boarding school that I must attribute at least a portion of the philosophies that I am about to expound upon in this book on my thirteen to fifteen year old experience at this school.

The budget got tight for my parents at home and my dad got a new job further north in the city of Burton Upon Trent (the center of the brewing industry in the UK) and we moved house to a city called Litchfield. I had to leave the boarding school in Guernsey and I was enrolled back into the public education system on the mainland in the UK in Litchfield, only this time I had passed what was called O levels at boarding school and was actually back up to speed with the other kids of my own age group. On the strength of this success I was able to go to a grammar school in Litchfield and this time I was going to be with the potential winners in society (what a system!). I was no longer doomed to the trash truck route, but instead I was directed towards a white-collar job in provincial UK!

Going to a school like this from a private boarding school was a no no in England, because there is also a very strong class system and it is bred into kids at a very young age. I dreaded any of these kids finding out about which school I had come from and then making my life Hell. This even included some of the teachers. When asked what school I had come from, I used to omit the last one and tell them I had come from Africa, and that I had come up from Sussex, which always interested them. They bought that again and again. I learned to make friends with a totally different breed of kid. Again, I made lots of friends; from necessity I learned to mix with many and avoid the others. I found that wealthy or poor, certain individuals are cast in life to be the good guys and others not so good! Some are warm, friendly and pleasant, and others are cold and gloomy or icy and aggressive. You name it, there are people who fit all circumstances!

Well the rest of my education was somewhat uneventful and college passed with many experiences both good and bad. I think during my whole education period in my life, the one thing I learned really well was how to make friends fast and also how to assess who were the good people to be friends with and who weren't. What I gained from that experience is learning the art of three minute analysis, or weighing a person up in a very short period of time on the first meeting. Believe me, it is a great skill to learn, especially if you are a salesperson!

During college, to earn spending money, I worked in many fine restaurants and hotels as a waiter all over the UK, and when I did eventually go into the work force, I joined a large hotel chain as a management trainee. I was transferred from location to location all over the country, going to hotels that had different specialties. For example one had a very busy bar business, another had a Cordon Bleu kitchen, another specialized in banquets etc. I had great hands on training, but was lonely really, because you were never situated anywhere very long. Again my ability to make friends fast paid off and so I left friends at every stop and enjoyed the experience greatly.

I met my wife during this period in my life and it was and remains to this day the best and most meaningful decision I have ever made. From the first time we met I made up my mind that this was the woman for me and was not proven wrong.

During this time I got a rupture lifting a keg of beer and had to be located to the head office of the hotel chain to recover after the surgery, so my wife and I made a home in a modest rental house nearby. We couldn't afford to live on the money I earned so I quit the job and went into Real Estate, not quite like the Real Estate business in California where I live now. The job was offered to me on the first interview with a salary, no commission, but barely enough to pay the bills. My wife got a part time job at a factory making coin rejecters for slot machines and we struggled on. I very quickly became the top closing salesperson in the company, much to the jealousy of my compatriots in the office who had for the most part been in the business for years. I attribute my success entirely on my ability to deal with people and make friends. The job lasted about eighteen months and when I could not stand working without commission anymore I went to the owner of the company and asked him to give me commission and he refused on the grounds that the others would be upset if he did. I left and the story continues.

I left the area with my wife and moved down to the Southwest of England and opened up a Real Estate office with my brother and we did quite well. But I wanted more. To give you an idea, the total money we used to get after all was said and done, for selling a home in that part of the world, amounted to between $150.00 and $350.00 depending on the home. I had heard that things were considerably better in California and that Real Estate commissions were in the thousands of dollars on each deal. So one evening while my wife and I were at the kitchen sink washing and wiping the dishes, we made a decision to move to California. Thirteen months later we arrived in California with our three children and three large trunks. We had sold everything else before we left England. We got our immigrant visas and started our new life. Perhaps in another book I will tell you the story of our early days in California.

The American people were wonderful and the life was unreal to us. I got my Real Estate license after about seven months and went to work. Soon we were on a fast ride to success. I was selling homes and I enjoyed the people and we were making money based upon my ability to make friends with people. It was great.

I joined a company that was affiliated to a National Franchise organization in Real Estate; the company itself had many offices and had about 750 agents working in those offices. I was rooky of the year in my first year, top in listings the second year, second in total sales that year also and top in sales several years thereafter. It was great, only to be topped in my third year with the company by being awarded a coveted top ten salesperson nationally by the National Franchise organization we were affiliated with. I was in the number seven position in the nation with an organization of over 1500 offices and over 35,000 agents nationwide. What an honor! It was really working for us and it was all credited to interacting with people in the right way, and of course hard work. I guess I can attribute a lot of it to my "persona" at the time also.

Kindness in words creates confidence.
Kindness in thinking creates profoundness.
Kindness in giving creates LOVE.

                                                            Lao Tzu

Chapter 9

Your "Persona" And Your Career.

First of all I want to reinforce a thought," you work to make money". Your career choice should involve your personal goals for having a meaningful life, if you can incorporate the two in a career choice and derive personal satisfaction from the choice then you are on to a winner.

During my life I have tried my hand at many different kinds of work, some successful and some not so successful, I first left College in England and was lost initially as to what career choice I wanted to make. My father was a master brewer at the time. He was one of less than 200 in the world with that high a brewing qualification, a man of cool disposition but a strong, honest, wise person with singular mindset. I remember one day just after I had graduated with a Business degree, he asked me what I wanted to do now that I had finished College. I really had no answer. I had always loved visiting the different brewing establishments that he had worked in and just didn't see myself as good enough with chemistry to go into his field of work, I did however always enjoy my times working with people as a waiter during my College vacations and weekends as a temporary silver service server at banquets for a catering company. I had also served at various different bars in hotels and found enjoyment meeting different people from all parts of the world. The issue I had with the question was that I really had no idea and I knew that my father was giving me a nudge that I needed to get my act together and make some important decisions. He pointed out to me the things that had appeared to interest me during the previous teenage years and offered to introduce me to his company's affiliate vice president who was managing their hotel division where he suggested I could specialize as a chef or hotel manager trainee or at least something in the field of people service. Well I didn't need much persuading, I had no better thoughts on what I wanted to do and within a few days

I had an interview, was hired as a hotel management trainee and was immediately posted to a hotel where I was to learn the specialties of a gourmet kitchen under the supervision of the foremost Escofier chef in the hotel chain. The experience was rewarding in so many ways, but I never really saw myself as a chef as much as I enjoyed cooking and I might say, the learning experience has always been a good one ever since, when my wife and I eat in fine restaurants I can always define the quality of the chef by his sauces and presentation and even the diversity of his menu. It was a plus.

The management training program involved a six month stay at different hotels in various locations around England with the objective of learning from their best at a facility that specialized in that particular part of the business. My next posting was to a small but very intimate hotel/pub in the Cotswold's in the middle of England where the training involved bar keeping and cellar management, in this job I enjoyed an enormous responsibility, because my role was to manage some of the oldest wine collections in the hotel chain, some bottles being very expensive and all requiring turning and cycling, it also involved learning how to manage wooden Bitter beer barrels which is a fascinating art, unlike caring for keg beer that is so common throughout the world today.

When the beer is initially delivered it has some hops in the barrel, there is a measure of finings which is a clarifying agent that is added to the beer and even a little yeast. It is cloudy from all the rolling and pushing on the truck and then down a ramp below ground level to a cool cellar where it is stored on a rack to stop it rolling. As soon as it is delivered, a tap is hammered into the bottom of one of the sides through a wooden bung which is installed at the brewery and a little shive or conical shaped bung is driven through another plug which is located in the side of the barrel and then the barrel is left to settle for about 7 days.

Once the bar is ready for more beer the barrel is tapped and that means a beer line is screwed onto the tap and the little shive which has been rotated to be on the top of the barrel lying on its side, is lifted just a little to prevent a vacuum forming in the barrel as the beer is pumped by hand at the bar. That is why in English pubs you often see them pumping the beer.

Well now you know how to keep beer in a cellar, let's move on! During my stay at this hotel which was located next to RAF Croughton in Oxford shire, this was a US Air force base not far from Upper Heyford a much larger US Air force base, it was here that I got to meet so many nice locals and it was my first real one on one opportunity to meet Americans in this particular case American soldiers serving overseas. I immediately took a liking to most all of the Americans that came through the bar and restaurant at this hotel. Looking back I always wondered what it was about the Americans that was different to other nationalities and I think it is only since I came to live in America and have done for over 26 years, that I realize that the American People are a fundamentally generous and easy going people with a warm disposition to foreigners especially when they are in foreign territory. They are generally great emissaries and give a very good impression to others. Having said that, I don't mean that all Americans have warm "personas" but what I do mean is that they usually make an effort to improve their "personas" when in foreign territory. This is a truly good thing and should be applauded as a good National characteristic, if only it could be carried on more at home.

While posted at this Hotel, I also experienced the boss from hell. This was a woman who for whatever reason could not take responsibility for her own mistakes and failures and blamed every member of staff constantly for what were fundamentally errors in management and her cool "persona" over spilling on to those who were unable to fight back. Even when not on duty she was a as true a "Blue" as I have rarely seen in a person and I would love to know what lay in her background, something haunted her and I know she didn't really like being that way but just couldn't help herself at the time, a sad story.

During this time of management training I met so many great people at every location I was posted to and yet I was lonelier at this time in my life than at any other time. To pinpoint why, I can only think that it may have been because I knew that all the relationships that I made were short lived and that I would soon be moving on and they would become past tense and I think my soul knew that and somewhere I only let the friendships become superficial which on the surface felt good, but down below the surface I was building a wall and that may have been adding an inner blue to my "persona" I am not sure that it showed that much because I think I had learned to conceal my true emotions years ago in my school days. I hope you can understand what I am saying here, it is life's circumstances that affect us on a day to day basis and we live with them even though they may be having an effect on us inside and we can sometimes give an impression as I did at work, that everything is just rosy in the rose garden, when it is really flowering weeds and they are trying to strangle the roses from blooming.

I left the hotel business after a couple of other postings, primarily my reason was because the hours were enormous, over 100 per week, and I also got a rupture lifting a keg which incapacitated me somewhat and so I decided to move into a different line of business and joined a Real Estate Office. , It was a three office family-owned company and employed about three salespeople per office. I took a job as a trainee salesperson, no commission, a small salary but still dealing with people, stability in one location and a wife and two children to support. I thought I had it all! I sold houses like there was no tomorrow and enjoyed every minute of it, soon I outsold every other salesperson in the company. During this time at work my wife was bringing up the kids in the daytime and at night however, she went to work at a gas station pumping gas for a while and I watched the kids at home. She then decided to change jobs and went to work in a factory that made coin rejecters for slot machines. Life was tough and it was about to get tougher.

We rented a small home in a row of homes and we still couldn't earn enough to get off the poverty level. Together, we agreed that I needed to get more money on the day job and I went to the owner of the company and asked him if he would pay me commission. He couldn't do that, he said. If he gave all his people commission I would be earning more money than any of his seasoned salespeople and he could not let that happen. So I quit there and then joined the unemployed. I went from place to place with no luck. After about four or five days, I found a job at a steel factory and it paid more money than before, only the job involved more working hours but included overtime when necessary. I used to start at 6.00 AM and worked most days until six or eight o'clock at night; my job was to haul strip steel manually in from the yard where the truck dropped the loads and stack the twenty foot lengths into the racks indoors and when I wasn't doing that, I dipped baskets full of pipe hanging clips into open tanks of red oxide which had been diluted with industrial thinners. After about an hour or two of this I would get dizzy with the fumes and have to take a fifteen minute break to clear my head again before going back in to continue the work. If anything was going to make my "persona" blue, it was that job. At night after I finished that job in the day time I would go home and spend between one hour and two hours at home with my wonderful wife and then I would go back to work at a night club as a bouncer which was from 9 o'clock until 2 AM and then home to sleep. This lasted for over eighteen months and the reason it lasted as long as that was because I couldn't take time off to look for another job. We were trapped and things were bad, really bad. Well you might think we had problems at home with that kind of lifestyle. The answer is yes and no. We loved each other a whole lot and we both knew that things would improve someday. We had hope. We did however have arguments and I think I was primarily to blame because I was so fatigued almost all of the time and I was short-tempered because of it and I really knew it deep down. What good came out of this? We made two of our very best friends who are still our longest standing best friends. We learned how we did not want to live and we always had hope. Our relationship was strengthened beyond any superficial rose-colored glasses relationship and we never quit!

I have not really talked about our "personas" during this period for several reasons. First of all, I never thought about "personas" then, and secondly, I had only one goal in my mind in those days. I wanted to be a millionaire so bad I could taste it and even in the depths of those dark times I never gave up the dream. I just knew that it would happen one day and that was enough. So what about our "personas?"

I think that my wife got hit the worst during those times. She had to have blind faith in me and my ability to pull us out and she also had the tough job of going through another pregnancy (the third) pretty much alone. She was violently sick through almost all of the pregnancy and had no one to be there except our dearest friends Keith and Lin who were our friends then and who gave us the strength of LOVE when we really needed it. I was always at work including weekends at the day job and she spent almost every day confined to the house with no spending money, or credit cards and three kids to bring up on her own. Life was really tough. When I hear mothers today whine about not getting a babysitter or expecting their parents or In-laws to baby-sit I just keep my mouth closed. We never had that privilege, yes PRIVILEGE and whilst I don't begrudge the youth of today having such an easy life as a whole I do think that it wouldn't hurt any of those with a good life to experience a little discomfort for them to realize what it could be like and so appreciate what they have even more, when parents and In Laws baby-sit, it is because they LOVE to not because they are expected to.

I know there are many people today that are going through their own hell and I say to all, you must have hope and a dream and focus on it every day like a life blood until you attain your goal.

So, how were our "personas" I think I can honestly say that as strong as we both are as people, we were cool with warm patches, what do I mean by that? We are both warm "personas" in different ways, but during these times, things were so tough that we burned cool or blue and it was our true inner warmth that really pulled us through these times, some scars? Yes quite a few, Good or bad? Both I think some gave us special strength to handle other major events in our lives and others we carried forward for a long time, more internally than externally. I do not recommend extreme hardship to anyone; however I do say that extreme hardship can bring maturity to a person beyond most others if the hardship is handled head on with undaunting courage. To get past it no matter how bad it gets and the experience is filed in the "bad" experiences folder of our "persona" with the additional folder of "lessons learned" being filed there also.

As our lives moved forward we decided to move closer to my parents and my brother who lived in the extreme Southwest peninsula of England in the County of Cornwall, a tourist area and a more relaxed environment than where we had lived previously. I went back into a Real Estate office working as a salesperson, and sold many homes there; from there I joined my brother in partnership in a Real Estate company we formed together and we sold homes for a while there together. During this time I was restless, I was never going to achieve my goal of becoming a millionaire if I stayed there and one night after dinner, while my wife was washing the dishes and I was drying them, I for some reason wiped the same dish twice and she asked me what I was thinking about and I asked her if she would consider emigrating. To my surprise she didn't miss a blink and said "where do you want to go?" We talked about Australia, New Zealand, America, Florida, California, and we both decided right there and then that we should sleep on the thought and see how we would feel in the morning. The morning came and we made the decision to immigrate to California. The agreement was also reached, that if after two years living there, if either of us was not happy, that we would come back with no questions asked. That was it! Spontaneous, yes but a decision we have never regretted; the two years passed and we both passed it without even a second thought. Years later we brought that up in conversation and we both agreed that it was not even a slight issue; we both love it here in California.

When we arrived in America, I was mind boggled with the American way. As soon as I got off the plane, we left the airport and I couldn't get over the size of the streets and all the big cars and how luxurious the cars were. I remember looking at the homes and thinking how organized the streets were with lots of single story residences and the enormous choice of eating places; the concept of a fast food place was just out of this world. I remember the choice of products in the mega-sized stores and the wonderful way that streets were laid out in uniform rectangles like a great big checkerboard. Were the streets lined with gold? Yes they were, only you had to know how to find it.

This was the mind-set that we arrived with in America, Three children, three large trunks of clothing and the clothes we had on our backs. It was scary, exciting, and adventurous and we both knew that there was no going back. I went through a couple of jobs when we first arrived, I took a job as a plumber's assistant within a week of arriving, then I sold eleven foot long sail boats, the car top variety and all this was while I studied for my Real Estate license.

Once I got my Real Estate license I felt like a racecar at a grid start to the Indy 500 I was ready to go and go I did, as soon as I got it. I won't go into all the specifics but if you had tried to feel the warmth of our "personas" during this time, you would have got burnt. Let me tell you it was amazing. Our story of emigrating here is a book unto its own and maybe one day I will sit down and tell you our story; for right now, I want to talk about people in sales positions; they are a major part of the work force, they earn money usually by some form of incentive and can become enormously wealthy if they are in the right job with the right incentives.

What makes a great salesperson? I think I know what makes a great salesperson. During my life as a Real Estate salesperson and broker, I have had the privilege to work with the very best in the industry and I have also watched many fall into oblivion. Many of those that fail are nice people with good intentions for the most part. They have a dream of being successful and they also make the commitment to work hard at it and yet they still fail. What is it that distinguishes success from failure? I think that it is for the most part their "persona" and how they apply their "persona" to their routine life in sales. When I first joined an office of high performers, I felt electricity in the office every time I went to work; it was like warm orangey bolts of energy were bouncing around the room. Everyone who was in the office was successful to their own level of success and everyone emitted an energy of their own. It was nice to be around such warmth. It wasn't the office environment, it was the people themselves. It was their focus and their energy as "personas" that made things happen.

You may well ask was everyone a warm "persona?" No not at all, in fact there were several "personas" in the office that were the "doom and gloom" brigade but the overwhelming warmth in the office, to some extent overpowered even their gloomy "personas" if nothing else it brought their color to a neutral tone. No two people worked the same way and no two people had the same personality and yet as individuals they were all successful salespeople. I believe that the infectiousness of the "personas" together in the office caused each and every one of them to glow a little more than they might have done on their own and in a work sense, the work ethic was influential also; they all created prospects and leads their own way and their "personas" individually enabled them to achieve success in their presentations according to their abilities. In offices where the "stars" are isolated into their own private quarters, the energy emitted is closed off and the other producers or non-producers are left to their own devices and to live off their own "persona's" energy which if cool in the first place is not very motivational.

On occasions when I have been in the presence of a group of sales people at a meeting or a conference, it can be with mixed vibes and the reason I believe it can have variable impact based on the content of the meeting is based upon whether the "personas" in the audience bring coolness or negativity with them. It is a fact of life that in a group of people there will be warm and cool "personas" a lot of the time it depends on the speaker or host to determine the warmth of the room in "persona" terms. If they are able to at least neutralize the cooler "personas" the overall success of the meeting will be judged by the warmth felt from the experience. It is not sufficient to have good content; it is the way the content is conveyed that ultimately counts. Most people go to meetings to not only acquire knowledge but also to feel warmth in the "personas" around them and many times the warmth they feel can be creating a false sense of security. They go, they get a warm experience, they leave and the fall on their face because the warmth is cooled drastically by the first cool "persona" they try to do business with or they allow their own "persona' to take over again. The feeling of cooling in those cases can be devastating and they just are not equipped to side step the cool breeze and blast it with their own warmth if they have any. The problem is that most people have no idea what their "persona" is like and cannot understand why people don't want to do business with them.

I am profoundly convinced that salespeople are what the marketing world needs to achieve sales whether it is homes or ice cream, the issue is that the people who become salespeople are there to influence others to buy the product. It really doesn't matter if the item is a home or an ice cream bar, if the salesperson is really a salesperson then they can sell either without very much training at all, just give them the pen and paper to sign up the deal and you will find that a true salesperson can do the job obviously training in that particular field of sales is very important but what I am eluding to allows for the fact that a salesperson has product knowledge.

Whenever I recruit a person into my business as a salesperson, I usually know whether they will be able to do the job before I hire them, so why do I take them on if they don't display those qualities? The reason I do that is because sometimes their real "persona" is hidden inside their façade and it may take a little while for them to display their true qualities; everyone deserves a chance! The first sign of a non-salesperson is the person who wants me to list all the crutches I have available to them. What do I mean by crutches? I mean tools of the trade that have been developed by large companies to help the inexperienced and incapable make at least a modest livelihood. My initial response to anyone who takes offense at that remark is to take the challenge. Give a top producer in any business a task to sell a "whatever" and give a low or non-producer the same task without any tools of the trade and see who gets the job done. You may well say that you have to have tools to do a proper job. I agree completely, but my point is that if there is no ability in the first place there will never be star power until they make changes and it is not the tools of the trade they need to change, it is their "persona." Without a warm "persona" the success rate of a salesperson is going to be less than satisfactory. Once a salesperson has sold all their friends and relatives, the true depth of their success is to be seen by their sales to strangers; for sure they will need all the warm "persona" they can muster.

Where does a "persona" influence a sale? In a sale situation, the buyer or customer is looking to buy (let's call it) a widget and the salesperson has a widget for sale. Often a customer will not buy that widget even though they want it, and the converse of that applies also. A salesperson has a widget for sale but it is not the color that the customer really wants but they buy it anyway. Well what makes that happen? I think that the customer is influenced in both scenarios by the "persona" of the salesperson. If they come across as pushy or arrogant or rude or depressing or talk too much all these are statements of a salesperson trying to control a cool "persona" in a warm direction and it doesn't want to go there and ultimately it comes out as an un appealing sales job. On the contrary in the second example the customer doesn't like the color but it is a widget and the salesperson is emitting a warm, pleasant, nice, friendly glow and so what, the color isn't that bad and the salesperson is great why not? It happens all the time. Have you ever found that you tried to persuade someone to do something and subconsciously you were down and the other person just declined your persuasion? Then on another occasion you are just bubbling and in such a good spirit and the person just said yes because you were so irrefutable? We have all experienced it. Sales is no different, it is so important for people to understand that it is not always what you say but how you say it and how other people see what you say in your demeanor rather than your actual statement. That is why I made the statement that it doesn't matter what you are selling; it is how you go about it that counts.

Years ago, when I first arrived in this country and I was selling residential listings and sales, I used to get prepared for my appointment in the office by getting all my paperwork together, but I would never make up a presentation folder. It seemed to me that it was an unnecessary distraction and I wanted to see the color of everybody's eyes at all times during the presentation. What it really was, was that I wanted to read their disposition as I did my presentation and if it was a husband and wife, I wanted to see who was dominant and who I needed to focus on more than the other in order to succeed. On the way to the presentation, I used to turn on my car radio, put my favorite song into the cassette player and blast the car out. In those days it may have been ABBA, or that song from Rocky "Eye of the Tiger." By the time I got out of the car at the home where I was going to do my presentation I was cranked up on such high warmth inside, no one was going to say no and most times that was the case. You can't win them all but sure can give it a try, RIGHT?

A "persona" in any business situation is so influential, in management, a warm "persona' can achieve what cool "personas" can only dream about. What do I mean by that? I mean that a warm "persona" commands loyalty, better production; it encourages a team spirit attitude among subordinates. As long as the "persona" is mingled with good rational common sense in the decision making processes it will work amazingly well. A cool "persona" on the other hand can create distrust, bad work ethics, and loss of respect. It is all created in the minds of the beholders; in this case it would be the subordinates. In an office environment, all it takes is for a cool "persona" employee to start bad-mouthing management for any reason and it can create a completely unacceptable work environment for otherwise warm "personas" around them. It is contagious and not part of a working atmosphere. If a person feels these feelings of discontent, it is much "warmer" to control them publicly and voice their discontent at the person responsible in private or quit if it is not changeable, the key to the whole issue of work environments is to be as warm as possible at all times, after all we all spend much of our lives in a work situation and if you are retired you have already paid your dues and I am sure that you will agree that a warm "persona" is a much better "persona" to be working with.

While we are thinking about careers and how our "personas" affect them, let's discuss those of us who use our hands to do physical labor and how our "persona" can impact that kind of worker in the everyday scheme of things. First of all, I think that people who are involved in physical labor can be the most sensitive to how a co-worker's "persona" may impact them. The very act of doing physical labor can be either very rewarding if one is healing or building something or it can be very tedious if the work is very repetitive and back breaking in its nature. Particularly in cases where the work involves strenuous activity on a daily basis, it is easy for a person to become irritable or bored especially if the job is repetitive and it is the bored people that emit those cool or blue auras when they are around others. Many times it happens because they are not pushing their own abilities to the test and they can feel insignificant or downtrodden or just plain fed-up. The question is why would anyone who feels like that even want to make a change to a warmer "persona"? There are many reasons I can think of, how about just making life feel better as a whole, taking everyday boring events and turning them into interim events waiting for something better to come along, after all nothing is going to change unless we make an effort to change them and there is nothing that I can think of that will enable that change to take place than working on a warmer "persona". Life is what we make it! If we want to be boring then let's not do anything about it, is it fun being boring? No of course not, so why put up with it. At work, if a person is doing tedious physical labor and it is really arduous, perhaps I can suggest using ones imagination during those particularly hard times of monotony, dream of what you would like to do in your life. Dream of good, nice things that you would rather be doing and make a plan to change things if you can as soon as possible. Should that decision be too difficult to do at the time, then you must accept the circumstances as o.k. and make every effort to create a different work ethic, one where you can resign yourself to be the best at what you are doing that you can be and don't look at your job as mundane, find the big picture and make it's relevance important.

I always remember the day I was in a parking lot of a local Supermarket and in the parking lot was an employee who had been assigned to bring in the shopping carts, it was a blistering hot day, one of those where being outside was probably an intolerable option if someone had a choice. This fellow was performing the job with zest, wishing passers by to have a "Good Day" offering assistance to those ladies who were struggling with the week's groceries to load them in their vehicles and to look at this fellow; you could feel that he was giving it his all. I remember thinking to myself, he is the president of his company, he is a true winner, he wasn't judging his role, and in fact he was singing when he wasn't helping someone or wishing them a good day. I bet no-one else in the staff would do the job or were moaning about doing it. It is how you do things and how you affect others that count and it doesn't matter what kind of job that you do. Be happy that you have a job and then strategize your growth plan from there. If you are feelings trapped in a job, then get an exit strategy together for improvement and stick with the plan. Without a plan in life there can be no path to success. If you have a job think about the fellow I just described to you and make every effort to be proud of that job no matter what it is and make yourself a person who others can look up to, I certainly felt proud to have watched someone who did such a menial task with such enthusiasm and pride. I hope you are feeling my message more and more as we go through the chapters. Life is so good, everything we do can be good, even when they appear to be bad and tedious, we still need to look for the positive side of the experience, for sure there is something positive to be got from just about any experience in life and in ones career there is such variety of labor choices it is hard not to find something that we could enjoy.

Years ago when I was a teenage student working a vacation job with a furniture removal company, I remember that this was just the toughest physical work, lifting huge pieces of furniture up and down multiple flights of stairs. This was back breaking work and I remember one day I was working with this crew of three other men who I had been assigned to work with that summer and we had the task of lifting a grand piano from a third story room down to the street to pack it into the removal truck. This thing weighed several hundred pounds and we each had to do the best we were capable of in order to get it down the stairs in one piece unscratched. I remember the first time I had to lift my quarter share of this load, thinking that it was an absolutely impossible task (that was before I learned that nothing is impossible if you set your mind to it) I just wasn't set in my mind that we could do this. The three other guys consisted of two large burly chaps who stood about six feet or so tall and a third man who was an Irishman about five foot eight tall, thin, wiry and who had a leather back support around his midriff. I remember the other guys saying their heave ho type of encouragement and the Irishman not only taking his own load but also trying to help me with mine, he said "c'mon laddie we can do it, one step at a time o.k.?" I remember his words of encouragement as he spoke and then he said he had had two hernias in his life doing removals and that if I was to lift even harder I could have one also. I remember us all just laughing at the top of the stairs and then we set to the task. We succeeded in getting that monster down to the street and into the truck I lifted like I had never known how and when we completed the task, I asked "Paddy" why he kept doing this kind of work if he had sustained such injuries doing it, His answer was simple, he said that he knew no different and he wasn't about to learn now. I guess he had found peace with his job; it wasn't his dream job but he made the most of it with levity and pride. I gained so much from his brief friendship. Thanks "Paddy".

The people we meet performing our career choices are varied and diverse and I must say that too often we don't appreciate the lessons that others can teach us, not only about ourselves, but life and the benefits of other people's opinions and experiences, too often we don't take the time to listen when others are speaking. Or acting on other people's observations or experiences, they can be truly rewarding if chosen and absorbed in the right contexts. Our co-workers are a source of untold benefit; we need to appreciate that always.

On another occasion I was working in a hotel for a summer vacation as a waiter, it was a vacation town called Aberystwith in Wales, a coastal place where the people were friendly and the landscape around, beautiful. There were a number of us who had been hired to accommodate the incoming summer tourists and we all became close friends for a brief period and got to find out about each others life so far and interests etc. Amongst these people were a couple both in their early twenties, very much in LOVE, why they were there I have no recollection, but I got to know them quite well, he was a tall lean sort of a guy with an ugly temper and an equally unique face, she was very every day no major physical attributes of note, except she was the nicest person you could wish to meet, They were employed as dishwasher and pot scrubber in the kitchen of this large hotel. At night after work, we get together in the staff room which had a piano in the corner; we would talk for hours on various subjects almost every evening. Then one night, the woman said to her boyfriend, "why don't you play one of your tunes for us?" I love to hear people play musical instruments and I encouraged him also.

What followed can only be described as a spiritual and physical explosion of my senses. This man sat down and made that piano produce sound of extreme rhythm that I have never heard again to this day, a sort of Jerry Lee Lewis/ Roger Williams rendition completely invented by him and to crown it all, he had never had a lesson in his life of either music or piano. I can't tell you how often I asked him to repeat his rendition on subsequent evenings thereafter, it was just incredible. A fellow co-worker with a gift from GOD. Yet he was a mere dishwasher in a big hotel, who said there aren't any Angels?

My life has been filled with experiences like that and many of them are from people I have worked with, I think that we just need to open our minds to such experiences and notice them when they occur.

We must become the change we want to see.

Mahatma Gandhi

Chapter 10

Major Personal Tragedies And How They Affect Us.

This is an event of catastrophic proportions that occurs for some on several occasions in their lifetime. These are events that can change us forever and when they occur need to be handled by us individually in a variation of ways, because we are all so different.

I guess that addressing some of the major events that occur is not my priority right now; I am not at all the expert on these matters and don't profess to know how each individual catastrophe can impact a human being. My concern is how these incidents affect our "persona" and what safeguards we need to put in place to enable our "persona" to return to its equilibrium after an event of catastrophic proportions occurs in someone's life when very possibly their "persona" is plunged unexpectedly or expectedly to its lowest depths of blue or negative or frigid cool. I know at some time or other you have watched a surf program where the surfers are in Hawaii and they are riding those gigantic waves fearlessly, and then it happens, they lose control and the wave breaks over them throwing their body like a limp rag into the turmoil of water and white foam. Like that turmoil, the death of a LOVED one, or divorce, or loss of a home from fire or storm or earthquake or the contracting of a fatal disease and similar occurrences with the deep significance as those I just mentioned have a similar impact on the "persona" as the big wave breaking on the surfer. They are huge; we cannot control them and they throw us into a state of deep emotional stress, so strong that we are not always able to come up for air right at the time they impact us. This is so powerful that even our family and friends cannot help, at times like a death; the family may also be feeling similar devastation and is struggling to get a grip on reality itself, viewing the event from their perspective.

At the time the first shock wave occurs in our life, we need to let our emotions do whatever they need to do in order to find reality; this can take a long period of time and for those who are experiencing the pain of such an event, it needs to run its course. The "persona" of a person who is suffering grief or loss or extreme emotional or physical pain is not an issue to deal with in any way at the time of the occurrence. However as time moves on, it is equally important for all of us to understand that there is a time for healing any wound no matter how big the wound and the important thing is for us to recognize when the time is right to make a move towards reestablishing the "persona" to its rightful glow. The time frame involved in this healing process will vary greatly from individual to individual and so the choice of addressing one's "persona" lies with each individual according to his or her needs. At risk of offending some, I do stress that the sooner we can start the healing process the better, for to lie and dwell in the event that caused the turmoil no matter how catastrophic is to delay the healing process. Please note that I am not advocating forgetting the event as though it didn't occur; what I am saying is to try and find a pathway where we can learn to accept that the event occurred and our life is going to move forward anyway.

In order to warm the "persona" that has been plunged into such depths of cool so quickly and devastatingly, it is going to take a lot of TLC and administration of that TLC may lie on the shoulders of the one inflicted as so often happens in the loss of a LOVED one for example. No one else can take away the pain and it takes an enormous strength from within to take the first steps away from the tragedy. Take small steps daily; first of all find things in your life that are important, even if it seems insignificant at first, if it feels good do it. This is a time when you need to find your God's warm "persona" and wear his for a while.

You need to find peace and there is nowhere better than in the "persona" of GOD. So where do I find His "persona"? I suggest you start with a short walk, (by the way make sure you leave the cell phone at home) initially in a country setting, alone where you can here the birds and the trees and look out on the fields or a stream and talk with your GOD. If you don't believe in a GOD (I find that hard to grasp when you look at the incredible world we live in!) then speak with your own spirit, try to find a place in time that you enjoyed the natural beauty of the earth that we live on and meditate its beauty and how significant it is in your own life. If the ocean is available to you, go there, sit on a rock or go to a pier and walk to the end of it and look out at the sea and talk with GOD, tell Him how you feel and ask for His help, He is there to help and He really can hear you.

I can truly tell you that wonderful things happen to those who believe strong enough. It is times of extreme devastation that we all need a little help and to ask a higher power for help is certainly not as absurd as some would have you think. Take these therapeutic outings alone and often to start with, learn to enjoy the benefit of tranquility and the healing powers it offers to those who seek. I think that it is important to be somewhere peaceful, not in the home, where the expanse of nature can provide its most powerful energy on the broken soul. Take time, do not rush these experiences and use the warmth that you gain to help you through your daily tasks. As you feel strength take more ambitious steps, take a LOVED one with you or a friend, make a pact that the topics of conversation will only be nice warm topics and the things that are painful are left out of the conversations initially. Slowly build strength back into your "persona" by reading nice stories and doing things that please you; start building your calendar of events to a low level of volume initially and only calendar easy things for you to enjoy. As strength continues to build, do more things that involve a wider diversity of people mingling until you are back in the mainstream, always keeping in mind that you are healing still and any breakdowns are ok and perfectly normal, circumstances considered. Try to avoid moments of self-pity as time goes on. Initially it is normal and needs to be felt, but as time goes on it is important to get it under control completely. If it is left unchecked, it will definitely haunt your "persona" forever as will the grief if you do not find a path to release it. The suggestions I have made above are just that; they are suggestions and you may have a better idea, if you do then use it when you need it, but if all else fails and you want some escape, try my ideas. They are awfully therapeutic even when you just feel down. Other suggestions: walk face forward into a strong rain or wind, it sure cleanses the spirit. Sit on top of a high hill and look down on the earth below and feel the wonders of nature as a bird would see it.

I firmly believe that in our everyday lives, we really do not take the time to smell the roses; certainly even if we do occasionally, we don't do it anywhere near enough. For those who don't know what I am saying, you need a serious prod to get out there and do it. We have a beautiful world that has been given to us and we owe it to ourselves to enjoy the fruits of its beauty to the best possible way we can. During times of deep emotional devastation, we need to step out of our normal life and make a special effort to find our spiritual existence so that we can find a place deep inside like a well where we can start hauling strength from to recover. My suggestion to find a place where we can be one with nature is I believe a place that GOD gave us to draw on this inner peace and it is there in large quantities if we choose to look for it. I love to go camping and fishing out to sea miles from land and exploring remote places. My family laughs at me when I say I would love to have a place where there are no neighbors. Well I am not really antisocial, but I LOVE the tranquility of nature itself in all forms; it is truly a magnificent and awesome sight to see nature in so many different perspectives.

I have seen the Serengeti plains of Africa, The Victoria falls in Africa, the whitest beaches in the world in Mombasa, Kenya, the rich red soils of Zimbabwe, the Grand Canyon in Arizona, the sandstone wonders of Bryce Canyon in Utah, the red rocks of Zion in Utah, the serenity of the Lake District in England, The Scottish Highlands, the desert in Arizona, The Columbia River in Oregon, The Wasatch mountains in Utah, the trees and fields after an ice storm in Wisconsin, the Sahara desert in Egypt, the Bay of Biscay in a hurricane twice, The largest lagoon in the world at Aitutaki Island, a five acre atoll in the Pacific Ocean called Beach Comber Island where you can snorkel with some of the most beautiful species of fish imaginable and I can honestly say that there is no doubt in my mind that not only is there an incredible GOD who created them and there is no accident in the formation of the world that just made it happen like this. Each and every place I mentioned above and there are many, many more I have personally visited, is a masterpiece of creation and truly the greatest artist ever, created each one with loving tender care and to behold these wonders is a privilege and an honor. Gosh I can't wait to go on my next trip!!! To feel the passion of life in it's rawest state is the feeling that one needs to go to in times of deepest emotional pain, if you are unable to go there rent a movie or read a book about such places and as I said enjoy what the local area around you can offer, for so often we live in a place and never take the time to explore the area, Right? You know it.

Times of emotional devastation are a fact of life in some cases and a stroke of bad fortune in others. We are all destined to die and so are our loved ones and friends, yet when a death occurs, we are consumed by grief in the most part and the reason I said that is because as I wrote the statement, I thought about those incredible believers who can overcome their grief by their devout belief in GOD and that there is a Heaven. For those, my cap is off, I am afraid I am still working on that deep a faith and I go back to my thought, we are consumed by grief even though we knew it would happen some time. The problem is, we are not in control of the time it occurs, nor are we in control of the way it occurs, which means we are more often than not surprised when we find out it is going to happen in an illness or from an accident or other untimely happening and we react by having grief which I guess is the way that we feel when we lose someone very near and dear to us.

What is grief?

The dictionary describes it as: Deep mental anguish, as that arising from bereavement.

A source of deep mental anguish.

The question is can we control grief? I guess we can, as I have outlined above, the deep Christian believers can overcome its effects, because they believe that the dearly departed have not only gone to a better place, but they have also gone and are awaiting their own arrival next to them. With this thought, my challenge is that if we believe strong enough in a better case scenario that the loss effect of the death of an individual in one's life is reducible to some extent or in some cases completely. That is powerful stuff and it takes a bit of absorbing. If that really is true, then we need to find a way to reduce the enormous impact that a catastrophic event can have on us, in order to maintain our basic composure and "persona." I don't really know if we want that but wouldn't it be great if we could have that much self-control that we could handle even the worst events in our lives? I think so; it would enable us to recover easier, even if we allowed grief to go to a certain level of depth of pain and held it there, just enough where we could handle it better if not perfectly. I think it is possible, in the ways that I have described above, I think if we allow the awesome power of nature to become a part of us at the times we need help the most, GOD will come into our lives through his incredible creations and we can sustain a warmth that will help us to handle even the worst emotional catastrophes.

If you are having a hard time accepting my thoughts on this subject, I challenge you to come up with a better solution.. If you do, I hope that you will share it, because we all need help when it comes to this subject. There is no easy solution and I believe that my solution is gentle, peaceful and gradual in a time when nothing is important, loss is everything and inner tranquility is overpoweringly helpful.

Let's move on to perceived tragedies that are tangible: bankruptcy, loss of tangible assets, loss of job, and loss of worldly possessions.

I think that we need to put things firmly into perspective here, "money is not everything and it can always be earned again." In examining that last statement I want to suggest that we need to understand what part money and possessions play in our lives and how important it is to understand that in the BIG picture of life it is insignificant really. So what is important you may ask? How about LOVED ones, family, friends, health, food on the table, water for starters. Once we understand that these are the really important things in our life then riches and wealth and luxuries are all extras, "cream on the cake," What about a home? Of course a home is extremely important and we all need one, but is it more important than health or our LOVED ones? I don't think so. The real issue here is to understand that not having wealth is not the end of the world and there is always going to be an opportunity to survive even if it is not our dream choice. Most people in the Western world have lost sight of the fact that a major part of the world is starving and homeless and really, when we put things in that perspective a little discomfort of personal loss or demotion in the social strata is really nothing and should be handled that way. The "persona" of a person who undergoes this kind of loss is usually cool or blue and the impact of the loss usually serves to increase the intensity of the color in their "persona;" the color change is brought on by worry and stress.

Both stress and worry are factors that impact a "persona" deeply and negatively and must be handled with great care and enormous strength. Most everyone suffers from them and when in a devastatingly catastrophic event in ones life the volumes of both increase voluminously to such extent that they can completely overpower the whole "persona," and it is these occasions that we need to find a way to handle that overwhelming takeover or at least understand how to climb back out of the hole that it creates in our being. The whole issue of stress and worry is a factor in our lives even in the lesser routines of our life and to be able to handle them successfully in all circumstances is I believe a major step in learning how to have your own "persona" under control Like the devil himself, these two cohorts of his appear at all times and have a bad way of eroding even the most positive influences on our "persona," so that the net effect of a warming influence can be diminished to even a negative effect once it they have done their deed.

When we discuss the major events of emotional destruction in our lives I cannot think of an occasion when stress and worry are not present and so in analyzing this more seriously, if it is them that we feel in enormous extremes when we lose someone or experience a catastrophic event in our emotional lives, is it them disguised as what we call grief? Maybe, if that is so then we must take strong measures to find peace and tranquility and thus my suggestion that we look to nature for the solution. Is it also possible that the brother of grief and worry is cancer itself, this being the host that they both create in our bodies in which to manifest their control of our very being. Perhaps when we find the cure for stress and worry, we might be halfway to finding the cure for cancer. I cannot help thinking back to my childhood in Kenya in East Africa, a wonderful childhood I might add, but most importantly, I remember going into the African villages with the Africans themselves and their elders and I remember how despite their abject poverty that they were fundamentally happy people, quick to laugh at simple things, they derived great pleasure from their fellow villagers and loved to tell stories for hours on end. They sniffed a coarse form of snuff and rolled their own cigarettes from locally grown tobacco, ate fish and vegetables for the most part and yet the incidence of cancer amongst these people was to the best of my knowledge virtually non-existent. Why we ask is that? I think it was due to the complete lack of stress and worry in their lives and I also believe that we could all learn a lesson from the simplicity that they lived. Of course we can't live like primitive people, but we sure can keep our lives simpler in so many ways, less debt, smaller homes, more modest life styles, and simpler pleasures. All these contribute to the problem like heat on a pot on the stove and the more we have the more the burner turns up so eventually it boils over, if it is not checked it will boil over. Envision catastrophic events as a magnified situation of this example; it happens much stronger and much more violently on the "persona" and peace and tranquility are the handle that turns the flame down.

The "persona" is incredibly complex in so many ways and yet it is completely reactive to our everyday lives and thoughts and as much as it takes the path of least resistance, it can also be controlled by the human mind, by self control and determination and that is why we see in times of extreme loss like natural disasters people who are able to emit extreme warmth to others whilst their own losses may be the same or greater than the ones they are helping, it is within their very "persona" to be positive, warm and glowing orangey/ red hard to comprehend but true nevertheless, observe and learn from what you see, it may help you one day in a time of extreme need.

There are as many nights as days, and the one is just as long as the other in the year's course. Even a happy life cannot be without a measure of darkness and the word 'happy' would lose its meaning if it were not balanced by sadness.

Carl Jung

Chapter 11

How Do I Improve The "Persona" Of My Closest Ones?

The truth is that most people are not aware of their own "persona" and how it impacts the others nearest and dearest to them, we as human beings are a selfish breed as a whole and for the most part we really don't care much about what others think. Oh. Yes some do and those that do, sometimes care too much, so much so that they let it affect the way they live their own lives and that impacts their "persona" in a negative way often times to such an extent that it totally undermines their inner most being, which directly interprets into low self esteem, non confrontational submission to any and all circumstances and generally a negative type personality. These people are the quiet sufferers in society, often choosing not to mix very much with others in case they find confrontation of some sort or that someone might challenge their comfort zone or on the other end of the scale they become the bullies in society, too timid to confront the issues on their own doorstep, they choose dominance in circumstances where the others cannot fight back. A couple of examples of this type of personality is a boss at work or perhaps a customer in a restaurant in both cases they have dominance by situation rather than by their own strength of personality.

The first thing that needs to be addressed in this complex topic of our relationships is to understand when we are the true "persona" that we really are and when we are not or do we have variable "personas" created to suit the moment often founded in weakness. Sound strange? The point is that many people create variations to their "persona" depending on who they are with, for example the "persona" that is displayed at home can be completely different to the one at work or the one on display when out with friends.

As I have said before in this book, we are all influenced by the "personas" around us and the way we maintain the warmth of our own "persona" is to take control of our own "persona" in all aspects of our life. This means that we have to be completely aware of who we are and how we are at all times of the day. The reason that we can be different at home than at work, is because other "personas" come into play with different stimuli in different aspects of our lives. So it becomes apparent that ones own "persona" is definitely impacted more than is obvious by our relationship with others around us.

Keep that thought. Having accepted that others around us impact ones own "persona," so does your "persona" affect the others around you and it is that realization that we must use to create a positive, warm influence on those around your own sphere of influence. The impact of this will be strong and dramatic to those that are impacted at close range, but because it is positive in nature and one's aura is not something to be underestimated I can only say "have at it" it is powerful and it is influential in all the right ways.

So where does it start? It starts from the time you get out of bed in the morning, if you smoke, quit! It is a truly negative statement; it demonstrates that you do not have control of your own "persona". The reason I brought that up is because so many smokers light up as soon as they get out of bed in the morning even if the spouse does also; you have already started to make them think something is different without saying a word. If you don't smoke, do something that pleases you for about 30 minutes, be pleasant to your spouse or other half, do not say or do anything that is anything less than neutral on the fun to be with scale.

Think of good things that are going to happen in your day, do not think about existing problems during that time, worrying will not solve them, only positive actions will solve the problems, if your spouse is taking the hit on the problems, then be 110% supportive of their mental state, do not add to their pressures it is totally counter productive to demand attention if they are not showing any, attention needs to be earned by nice words and actions (positive stuff). If your other half appears to be in a bad mood at the beginning of the day, do not walk into the trap, yes it is a trap, if they are showing their bad mood to you, it may be because they want you to react either good or bad or alternatively they may be just mad and either way steer clear. Keep your positive thoughts going, do the daily routine, look at your notes or just meditate on the positive results you want for the day at home and at work. Many times the start of the day "persona" at home can be the "persona" that influences the whole day for not only one's self but everyone that comes in contact with it during that day. Be aware of this at all times, one cannot make a positive influence on the other "personas" around you unless you make an effort to make your own "persona" positive to be around.

Make bold positive remarks to everyone, like "you look happy today, has something nice happened?" "I love that dress or shirt" or whatever. Pick the right compliments for the right occasion, they count and when used correctly, they can make someone else's day feel really good. What a booster for their "persona" with such little effort on your part. Notice what a good job they did on some project no matter how insignificant it seems.

The art of improving or warming the "persona" of someone you are close to is not always easy. There are some prerequisites that may need to be present in order to have some element of success. First of all, you need to have frequent contact with this "persona" in order to influence them in a positive way. It probably wouldn't make much difference if you only spoke with that person once a week, although it is still a good thing to convey all the warm glow of your "persona" at any time you make contact, it certainly will make them think warm when they think of you and certainly that could make some influence. Imagine a pot of cold water and you have a burning match held under it really close, you have a tough job of warming the pot of water anyway with just a burning match, in time however it will start to work if the match is kept burning long enough right? Well that's the concept we are dealing with the others in your life you know that the pot will not cool as long as a burning match is held under it but it also isn't a quick process. For those that you don't see often or talk with often it is like pulling the match back away from the pot a little way this is going to have less impact than close up. You get my meaning I hope on this matter. Taking this analogy a little further, the warmer you can make your "persona" in your every day life style is like changing from a match to a propane torch for warming purposes it will in most cases have exactly that effect on those around you beware however, there is always a cool wind somewhere that cannot be expelled and that can put out even the warmest torch if it blows hard enough, Those are the "personas" that are so entrenched and closed minded that nothing will warm them, what do we do? We move to another room and close them out! It works, if you cannot make any impression on such people, then keep your own "persona" warm and don't let them get to you (shut them out emotionally in their own room!)

Let's just recap for a moment on this issue, we need to make sure that we have our own "persona" glowing as orangey/red as possible at all times in all situations, we need those closest to us to know that we notice them and that we care for them and how they look and feel at all times. We need to compliment them when appropriate and that needs to take place at least once an encounter or conversation if the encounter is longer than an hour then it should occur more than that even if an appropriate time does not occur. We need to notice what they say and listen to what they say even if we think it is inconsiderate or wrong, we can voice our disagreement but not too aggressively and move on to a more positive topic. No matter whom the other "persona" is, manners are always very important, show courtesy and manners to the others always without exception, this is one of the most powerful positive emissions a "persona" can feel and it is always a warming experience. No demonstration of manners is too small to display in any place at any time, remember that it is a BIG one.

Do nice things for them, make something with your own hands and give it to them, treat them to something, buy them a small meaningful gift, send them an appreciation card all these things count a lot and make good relationships GREAT and stressed relationships a little better each time you do something nice. Remember lots of "unconditional acts of LOVE"

I suspect that many men who read this will think that it is just not masculine to do all these things, men have to show dominance and masculinity and this is like sucking up and cowering down. If you believe that, you are destined to a life of misery. It is truly masculine to have the strength of "persona" to do all of these things and still be able to walk tall. In fact if one were to follow these principles to the best that one can, one would not only have control of one's own "persona" but most everyone around would be desirous of emulating just a little or a lot because all the things I am suggesting here are positive and respectful in all respects and adherence to the highest standards of behavior is nothing but good! Please note ladies that life is a two way street and you also owe it to your closest ones to respect and understand that they are to be treated with the same high standards and that means acknowledging any acts of courtesy and manners with a statement that shows you noticed and are grateful, so often I have seen acts of courtesy shown by men like opening a door for a lady or offering up a chair in a crowded room, go what appears to be completely unnoticed by a woman because she didn't say a simple "Thank You" how much does it cost to offer up these simple acknowledgements and even more important how much warmth does it add to all "personas" in it's perception range. Please note, that there is a huge misperception amongst married couples that after marriage all that "silly" stuff can now stop, it is no longer important to pay attention to such details. How stupid is that mentality? Attention all married couples, when people say you have to work at a happy marriage, it isn't just an idle remark, it is probably the truest under realized statement in the English language and any other language if it is used in them also. Why? The reason why, is because if all of the above were implemented into most marriages, I suspect that the divorce rate would be cut by 85% and most of those that don't go to divorce would also improve for just a few simple actions applied daily in everyone's lives. Ego, vanity, selfishness and greed are basically the common denominator that leads to failure in life. To remove or diminish any or all of the above from one's life will only serve to warm one's "persona". Obviously there are other factors that come into play, but these are some of the key players in the destruction process of any type of relationship and we need to be able to identify them in our own" persona" and then learn how to bring them into check and ultimately extinguish them from our "persona".

The application of positive attributes to our "persona" can be as big a challenge as removing the bad characteristics and may take years of constant attention to apply. All I can say to you is this "Never, Never, Never, Give UP!" They say that Rome wasn't built in a day and that also is true for our "persona;" it has taken a lifetime for us all to develop the "persona" that we have today and it certainly isn't going to take a few words in this book to make it change. This book, I hope, will serve as an awakening influence, one which will make us all aware of who we are and how we affect those around us. If the book succeeds in doing that, then I am happy, my goal has been achieved. The implementation is entirely in your own sphere of control and that is the hard part I know.

The influence that you exert on those closest to you should be objectively assessed by yourself before you implement any changes. The reason I say this is because it is important for you to be objective about your progress with them as time goes on. Be realistic about who they are and how easily they can be influenced and if you don't notice any immediate changes, watch their eyes when you do nice things, it always shows in their eyes! Don't give up too quickly, it's like pushing a snowball up a hill, too often people quit before they get to the top and that is only because the snowball was so big they didn't see that the top of the hill was just one more push away. Imagine all that effort going to waste just because we gave up too soon!

I want to address all those who are suffering with a relationship problem as they read this book. The relationship will not heal until firstly you get control of your own "persona". I know that is a pretty inflammatory statement for many who are blaming the other spouse for their short falls in the relationship, but hear me out for a minute. The reason that the other spouse is unhappy is because they are blaming something in your "persona" for their dissatisfaction. This applies to both male and female alike, it may be working too many hours, miserable to live with, not enough sex, too fat, too thin, boring, depressing, untidy, bad language, pornography, drugs, alcohol, incompatible, grown apart, mother in law, in attentive, disinterested and obviously a bunch of other reasons I have probably hit some of the major ones and any others I have missed, add them to this list. The point is this, we all need to look at the beginning of our relationship and objectively determine what the good things were about that other person that made us fall in love with them in the first place.

If you are the dissatisfied one then this part of the chapter applies to you:

It started good, in fact really good, and for whatever reasons it is not so good now, we blame many things for a relationship not working and often we go to counseling to find out what we already know but either won't admit to ourselves or don't want to say to our partner. Obviously there are other deeper reasons that need to be discovered in some cases and I am not qualified in any way to deal with those issues. However, I am a believer in reality and the truth is that many people blame their upbringing and other bad events that have taken place in their lives for the way they lead their lives today. At the risk of upsetting anyone who disagrees, I want to put some thoughts on the table for consideration.

When I was at one of the many schools I attended, I had the privilege of being taught by a teacher who had been a POW in a Japanese prison camp. He had been subjected to torture on a regular basis which included electrical shock treatment to his genitals. He had fingernails pulled out one at a time and a slew of other tortures which also included days of solitary confinement in a hole in the ground with a corrugated steel lid which was subject to intense heat in the day time. This man lived to see another lifetime of freedom afterwards and to be honest; it is remarkable that he was even sane, never mind able to teach a class of rowdy kids. The man was a peaceful, gentle, white haired and prematurely aged man, but a nice, nice man and a very kind disposition. Never did I hear an outburst of anger from him and never did I see him show any side effects of his ordeal in public. The point is, this man underwent horrific treatment in a time of war and for many, it would have destroyed their mental welfare; for him, not so, he was able lead a life with control of his emotions that one can only imagine what he must have felt inside. Self-discipline, it is a tough thing to learn to attain and often it is brought by true maturity. I asked him once if he had hatred in his heart and he looked me straight in the eye and said "if I did, I wouldn't be here." "Yes," he said, "I forgave a long time ago." That is true maturity. When you put a story like this on the table for scrutiny, it makes you think how pathetic most of the reasons above are for breaking up a relationship. How small are they compared to what this man went through? He went through torture and mental degradation and yet he found it in his soul to forgive everything and lead a new life afterwards with peace and contentment. In other words he was happy with his lot! I look at Senator John Mc Cain on TV and I think the same thing. He has undergone some terrible experiences in his life, but he has found it deep within his soul to carry a peaceful external disposition and he has picked his life very successfully and carried on. No one is saying that we can forget bad things that occur in our lives. I am sure that they don't forget either, but we learn to live with them and make the most of what we do have. I know this was an extreme example of how bad things can get, but I wanted to show an example of how people can be resilient to hardship of the most extreme kind and still come back and live life to the fullest. No, marriage is not a prison camp, but marriage can feel like a prison sentence to those who feel they are in a bad one and my point is that I think a lot of people get to feeling like the solution is to quit. I know there are some bad relationships that are just not fixable period because either one side or the other will not admit to their failings. It is not those that I am addressing here and I want those of you who are the ones in a relationship who are dissatisfied to take this path with me further. You need to ask yourself if you are fault free. If you said yes here, forget it, you are beyond help until you accept some responsibility for what is happening right now in your relationship.

The second thing to get straight is that good sex comes with a good relationship, so don't blame bad sex or no sex on the reason for the problem. If you have never had it good then work on fixing your relationship and abstain until it is the right time and that time will occur in almost every case when the relationship is on the right path. I think sexual incompatibility is one of the main reasons people use to break up a marriage and most of the time they cannot see beyond the end of their noses. It is the relationship that needs attention and accepting each party's responsibility for the cause of the problem would go a long way to fixing such a problem.

The third thing is to not find all the faults with your spouse. Look for all the good things and focus on those. If you feel that your spouse is the one who has changed over the time of the marriage, then try to understand what it is that has changed and why. Look for the causes of the break down. Once the true causes have been established make an effort to fix or heal the causes that you are responsible for. If forgiveness is required then apologize and mean it. Some mistakes may take time to heal and if they do, be patient and all the time make every effort to warm your own "persona" in the best way you can. The pairing of both may well be the cure to rift. If addiction is a cause then do what you need to do, accept full responsibility and find a cure with an honest commitment to yourself first then your spouse that you will not go back to the addiction and do it!

I think you can see that if you accept your own part in a failing relationship, then you are probably half way to a cure. The other part of the cure is taking the appropriate steps to make changes in your own "persona" that is desperately needed to improve the relationship. Remember your "persona" influences your spouse's "persona" and it always will so this is not a short term fix, you need to work at it ongoing in your whole life at home and at work and at play.

Let's move on to the victims of a bad relationship. First of all there is no such thing as a victim, it is a state of mind that you let yourself be in. If you want to be down trodden then you will be. If your relationship is failing then you must take a hold of yourself metaphorically speaking and make changes to your "persona". The causes can be many, lack of confidence, depression, shyness, perceived bad looks, (I put perceived because no one is ugly or bad looking throughout, we all have failings, some inside and some outside and we cannot dwell on such thoughts), feelings of indebtedness, lack of LOVE, self centered, egotistical, self righteousness and of course a host of other reasons. The point is that if you feel like a victim in your relationship and that things have changed since you first met your spouse, then you may well have changed just like them, except maybe in a different way.

We cannot live in the past; maybe the relationship has evolved into one of dominance and submission, which can happen over time, or maybe one of disillusionment or just mundane mediocrity through lack of effort on both parts, we need to accept the current state of the relationship, be objective with each other and make commitments to each other to make the changes deemed necessary to improve the relationship and a time frame should be built in to the commitment for reviewing the successes of the changes.

Influencing a close friend or spouse or relative, starts with oneself and if one makes a realistic, positive adjustment to ones "persona" in a focused way, it can be enormously powerful in its repercussions to the relationship just as a negative influence can be destructive and so often it is negative that overrides the simple lack of positive stimuli and thus a bad relationship it really is that simple, think about it! If you want a great relationship then cultivate it and make it GREAT!

Remember, you are the controller of your own destiny and it is for others to follow!

Why not let it be your spouse or sister or brother or friend? It is up to YOU!

The price of greatness is responsibility.

Winston Churchill

Chapter 12

Be Careful Of The Pitfalls In Making The Positive Changes

The time we spend on change is ongoing and forever, because we should always strive for our own self improvement, There is always room for improvement, the tough part is recognizing the "persona" characteristics we possess that need improvement and then being honest enough with ourselves to do something about it!

While we are on this aspect of improving our "persona" I think it prudent to grasp the true significance of this chapter. The way we live our lives, with our God, our family, our friends, ourselves and people and life in general, determines greatly our true inner happiness and along with that our own "persona;" it truly determines how our "persona" glows and this in turn reflects how we are really doing in our life. It should not be understated, we all have a standard that we live to in our lives, the standard that we accept is where it all starts and ends, if we do nothing to make improvement changes, then we will remain the way we are and if that happens to be a cool/blue state then that is the way we are and I was going to say always will be, but that is not really true, because the odds are that if you have a cool/blue "persona" it is more than likely that one's "persona" will find it very easy to trend cooler or darker blue, without a conscious effort or positive influence it is extremely unlikely to trend warmer or glow less blue. The real problem is that it is easy to glow blue if we let it happen, so that is the reason that it is an ongoing, forever commitment to work on self improvement in all aspects of our life.

To commit to change, one needs to work very hard at it initially, because it takes at least twenty-one days to create a habit and even then if the new habit is one that requires effort and devotion, it will be easy to fall off the wagon, so we need to make up our mind to make the changes we feel necessary and live with new changes.

I want to suggest at this stage that you read Chapter 4 again because the full implementation of Chapter 4 is the direction we need to point to for success in this endeavor. The "Middle Drawer" list is significantly important, make it as long as you can and add to it as you proceed with your life, move items from "My Dream Persona" list as you feel you have achieved success in a particular item on the list. Don't be too quick to do this however, while it is in the list of "dreams" it is highlighted as a need to achieve item and thus remains in focus and will not be taken for granted. However, having said that, if you really feel that you have mastered this item, to the point that you live it in your "persona" as a part of your life, then go ahead and add it to your "Middle Drawer" list.

The fact that you have made a "Bottom Drawer" list is a significant step in the plan and if you make a special effort to focus on good or positive events and thoughts when "Bottom Drawer" items loom into your daily existence you will experience an immediate improvement in your whole "persona" if you are able to keep the good thoughts in the forefront of your mindset. I think the "Bottom Drawer" items that have the biggest influence in your "persona" may well be items that have caused you deep mental scarring. The problem I am sure that you will experience with creating the "Bottom Drawer" is being able to not only put it in there but being able to truly remove it from your life. I cannot profess to have the answer to all the questions, but I do sincerely think that you must find a place of peace in your life that you can draw from when these things loom. For example learn Yoga, read the Bible or an excerpt from the Bible, listen to your favorite song, stop what you are doing and breathe in deeply, concentrate on the action of breathing deep and refocus your mind to what you are doing next in your day, refer to your calendar and remind yourself of the next NICE event planned in your life.

Whatever it takes, do it and work at it until you can put the item or items out of your immediate conscious mind; it is going to take time and patience and it will not be an easy path.

At the same time you focus on these changes in your life, make sure that you do some of the easier things on the "Dream" list. It is important to feel success as you strive for self improvement; it will help you to manage the tougher challenges with a much more positive mind set.

O.K. we have addressed the issues that lead to the plan in Chapter 4 and also what we need to do to implement those changes. Let's look now at the trials of achieving success and perhaps some of the attributes or skills that we need to develop in order to be a success.

Let us look at what influences would bring us to task on our path for success and I thought I would attempt to address some of these influences by letting you go down the path with me in ascertaining if you have the qualities to handle your own challenges. One of the things that I think comes to the forefront is;

Willpower; do you have the willpower to see this plan through to conclusion? The first question we need to ask ourselves is do we have a strong willpower? This question in itself is not an easy one to answer, can you live with a decision that you have made in the past that was very difficult to achieve, like give up smoking, lose weight, abstain from chocolate (this only applies if you have a sweet tooth), for those that are savory people, give up potatoes, you get my meaning now I am sure. Well we need to establish that we are tough enough mentally to follow through with the plan. It means taking lots of small decisions on a daily basis, check the calendar of events planned, and check the "Top Drawer" list at least four times a day. Make an assessment of each day's successes and failures at the end of each day and make a note of both. Make a special note of faux pas (little errors) that occur during the day to highlight the moments of weakness in your mind and recommit to a stronger attitude next time and keep moving forward.

The true success of the process is predicated on not giving up and it is that simple! To not give up is to have will power, the problem is that most people don't grasp that basic concept and end up giving up on basic life principles far too often and ultimately it is reflected by the color of their "persona" cool/blue. To have willpower simply means reaffirming your commitment to the plan on a daily basis, every morning, take a look at the mirror and say "today is going to be a great day" and make it that way.

Another powerful influence is temptation; can you say no to temptation? These are the events that occur on a daily basis, that influence us in a negative way and we allow them to infest our mind without any resistance. Some examples of these are, other people's weaknesses, they don't tidy up after them, they criticize you unfairly, they yell at you, they cut you off on the street, they do all kinds of things that annoy you or upset you, the temptation part is that you allow them to get to you and this affects your "persona" in a cool/negative way instead of just ignoring the stupidity of it and moving forward with your life. Just say "NO" to yourself, they will not affect my day.

The next very strong influence is our: comfort zone and it needs to be watched very carefully. Unlike willpower, our comfort zone really leans closer to "Selfishness;" in other words we allow ourselves to be cool/ negative "personas" because it is easier to be that way than it is to be a positive/warm "persona" that takes work and many of us are not up to the challenge. This is probably one of the most prevalent reasons in society for blue/negative "personas" and most of the time those that are like that just don't care enough to fix it and those that live around people with them allow them to carry on being that way. What a sad state of affairs and something that they should be ashamed of not proud of as so many appear to be.

Obviously our comfort zone is not always a negative thing but I still think much of its roots lie in the way I have described. In those instances where it is not a negative thing it still needs to be brought into check because we need to step out of our comfort zone in order to be able to improve ourselves and do things we may never have done before and be a little uncomfortable in order to achieve the desired success level.

An influence that you may not think about but will certainly be an issue if you come across it, is how others perceive you,

Your appearance to others: people see you now in a certain way and as you make positive changes to your "persona" you may become more popular with people and friends and this may have a negative effect on an already negative friend or spouse because of that old monster: jealousy. This is a burning passionate flame inside a person as I have alluded to before, but it is so incredibly destructive that it controls all the lives it is in touch with. Many of those who are jealous just don't realize how poisonous that emotion is and may be aware that they are jealous but just don't give the attention that it deserves to eradicate it from their lives. If you are making a strong effort to make your "persona" more positive and warmer, then you must identify the jealousy characteristics of yours or anyone who is in your life and learn to recognize the venomous comments that are made by these people and learn to put them into a place of peace. The venom of jealousy is worse than all the rattlesnakes and cobras put together and should be recognized as such. Be aware and in control always when a person has jealousy in their heart. They say and do things that just aren't nice a lot of the time.

Another influence to be aware of is complacency. It is the father of failure. Complacency is the attitude that creates a false sense of security, it is an attitude that puts one in a place of defenselessness and unpreparedness and ultimately if left unattended will lead to the downfall of even the strongest powers or people. Quite simply it means that we should never allow ourselves to think we are great or that we have a wonderful "persona;" it is completely negative and if we get to thinking we have it mastered, open the "Bottom Drawer" and climb in, because you will never have it with an attitude like that. Be aware of it and set it aside. A good biblical phrase I think applies here is "get thee behind me Satan."

Life's overall pressures are another influence that can harm or interfere with this process and we need to find special concentration to deal with these. The fundamental issue here is that we allow life's events to control our life and when we do that we call them pressures. If we are aware of what they are, we need to bring them into check or remove them from our life entirely. Most important of all we need to go to a peaceful place mentally when they are at their fiercest. When pressures are high, all the good things we want for our lives are sacrificed in favor of dealing with the pressures. The problem is that until we take control of ourselves the pressures will not go away. The moral to the whole thing is that you must fight even harder to make a more positive "persona" because the very act of self-improvement is a destructive blow to pressures. The killer blow is to identify them and get rid of them, face them or fix them by bringing them completely under control. Easier said than done you might say, well maybe, but I challenge you to read my statement again and act on it. It will work, you just have to have faith in what you are doing, and believe in it wholeheartedly.

Work is a place where many people spend a great deal of time and often do not have a lot of control on what happens in that environment and it also can have a strong influence in a negative way on the process of warming one's "persona." The fundamental reason for that is that we are in need of a paycheck and it is scary to put that in jeopardy so we do nothing to change what is happening to us there.

I know I have said this before but I mean it sincerely: change the working environment that you work in to suit you and your own plan (do the work of course, but make it pleasant to do the work) or alternatively take a big step and plan on making a career change or a work place change.

Remember, we only work to pay the bills and we owe it to ourselves to be happy at all times or as much as possible. God did not put you here to be miserable. Don't forget that. If you make the changes I have suggested, you will find the effect on your "persona" will be strong and dramatic and you will LOVE yourself for making the change and probably everyone around you will also. Obviously if you decide to change jobs, get another one lined up before you do it.

The strength of decision in the warming of your "persona" is a very important one; it is probably the most important decision you will ever make if you live rigidly to its principles. The process of self-improvement is a serious cause so make sure that you treat the decision that way every day of your life. There are pitfalls that you will encounter everyday, but the secret to success is to constantly be aware of how you are as a "persona" and what color your "persona" is glowing. If you can define the pitfalls as they occur and handle them with control and discipline, you will find the warming process to be very rewarding.

It is a lifestyle change and should be looked at that way, we cannot change overnight and it is not reasonable to expect that. It is reasonable however to make some immediate big changes, the ones like having good manners to others, to have a strong pleasant manner towards all people most of the time (there's always someone beyond help who we need to be negative with, just don't do it all the time if you have to do it, then do it well and move on! The key to this however, is that you do it with complete control of your own emotions at all times) Just being aware of your own demeanor is a major step forward and a reason for a pat on the back if you can institute this behavior right away and keep it that way. Be truthful on all occasions, the act of lying is a negative response or action and it has a much stronger impact on ones soul than one realizes, it metabolizes into guilt and remorse and that in itself is about as tough a knock as anyone needs to keep from becoming a more positive warmer "persona'

The changing of your own "persona" is more a case of true self control than almost anything else. It is the power to handle any situation without losing it and being able to make people feel at ease in your presence and feeling good in yourself because you feel good about your life.

The pitfalls are plentiful but if you take a very simplistic approach to everyday happenings and focus on the need to be positive in all circumstances and in particular, all thought processes, it will work for you in a way that you never dreamt possible.

In the next chapter I will address the situation of people who have or had the ability to influence thousands of people by channeling enormous amounts of internal energy into their "public persona" and yet still maintain a "personal persona" of their own. These different people have created a "persona" that affects the masses both white hot and icy cool in both extremes; the very impression that a powerful "persona" can have on fellow beings can be unbelievably exhilarating or incredibly destructive. Some people find a place in their inner "persona" to influence others in such a way that one could perceive their acts as one driven by GOD or the DEVIL himself and it is their ability to strike out into the "personas" of their fellow man that makes such people incredibly powerful and indelible in the hearts of those who watch from an influential position.

Beware who you break bread with for he/she may be the one to consume you!

Roy Taylor

Chapter 13

Inspirational Thoughts About The Power Of The "Persona"

During history we have heard about people who have immeasurably affected the human race and who have affected the course of history with their influence at the time. Have you ever wondered what makes one person come into the world just like any other and leave the world with an indelible mark of their presence? This applies to both good and evil unfortunately, but there must be something that distinguishes these people as different from all others and I am certain that it lies within their "persona" only with these people I believe they have something extra that most of us do not possess; I call it a "public persona". I think this "public persona" is something they are maybe born with, it is an ability they have within that allows them to channel extreme amounts of energy into this "public persona" and it is so powerful that it gives these people the ability to exert control or strong influence over masses of people, so much so that they can make people do things they have not done before or would never do had they not been subjected to the presence of such a person. I think that they must have the ability to channel such energy very early in their lives, and maybe many more have the ability than we realize, only a few learn how to channel it successfully into a state of extreme influence. To be honest I may be overstating the power, maybe it is simply the fact that these people have the ability to allow their aura to be felt more readily than others in a public environment I am not completely sure. However there is one thing I am sure of and that is their existence and the influence these people have had on the world. Some might call it achievement, others might call it power, or maybe just charisma, I believe it is because of their "persona" and the aura their "persona" emits. That is what gives many of these people the power or even the ability to achieve such incredible notoriety or charisma and it sure makes its impression on the world.

Let me name a few people both good and bad and I think you will
see a little of what I mean:

Jesus Christ
Cleopatra,
Alexander the Great,
Napoleon Bonaparte,
Sir Winston Churchill,
Pope John Paul II,
Mother Theresa,
Billy Graham,
Lech Walesa,
Nelson Mandela,
Adolph Hitler,
Mahatma Gandhi,
King Henry VIII
Julius Caesar,
Mohammed Ali,
Oprah Winfrey,
Rick Warren,
Madonna,
Elvis Presley,
John Wayne,
Bill Gates,

Obviously a whole lot more can be added to this list, but my main
point is to illustrate that each one of these people has made a difference
to a whole lot of people by being on this planet, I realize that there are
some very bad people on the list also but they have influenced the world
and will always be remembered in infamy for their acts and deeds.

The real issue is not really their deeds, the issue is that they have
all been gifted with the gift of notoriety and that notoriety came from
somewhere within and through their life and their actions in life, people
have placed them in a position of significance and given them notoriety.
I believe that when we think of any one of the people on the list, we
create a picture of that person particularly the more recent ones and
we determine on first thought their "persona" not the reason for their
notoriety. Let me illustrate my point-

Nelson Mandela: I think immediately of a warm, positive person.
I have no idea if he is like that but his "public persona" glows that way.

To have a warm "persona" after all those years of imprisonment, can you imagine what self control he must have?

Adolph Hitler: I just think icy cold, dark blue/black. He gave off that aura. I know his actions did for sure. He must have been just as cold personally, but he had the ability to use his dark/negative "persona" to influence an entire nation.

John Wayne: that guy was always warm in his aura and even the parts he played; maybe his personal persona was as warm? The all American hero, I think he used his own "persona" in his movie roles.

Oprah Winfrey: she is just glowing hot/ orangey red. I wonder if she is like that personally. I think so. I suspect that she has grown warmer and warmer with age and notoriety, maybe wealth also!

The point is that all of those who have influenced the world chose to step away from the pack; they took the world into their hands and ran with it the way that they saw fit, starting with GOD himself when he placed Jesus on to our planet. What an influence, to have his only son placed among us human beings with the sole purpose of influencing our very "personas" for decades to follow, did he succeed? You make your own call; I think he did in such a profound way that millions of people to this day live their lives trying to emulate the very teachings of Jesus and the "persona" that he chose to show. What an incredible "persona" he must have had!

This is a choice decision, it is within their very "persona" and some choose to use it and others who also possess it choose to subdue it in favor of mediocrity. Thank the Lord that those who have that Dark/ Blue/Ice Cold /Negative "persona" of a serial killer or mass genocide monster do not all come out into the open for I am sure that there are many more than the ones who we have become aware of that have been born that never took the choice to do what they were capable Likewise, those who have an enormous Orangey/Red/White Hot/Positive "persona" may never use it to the maximum potential they are capable of. The choice is one that people need to make in order to have the kind of influence the people on the short list above have achieved in their lives on the world and history.

The real question is do we have a "public persona" hidden within our "persona"? How do we determine if we have it? Is it accessible to us if we think we have it? What do we do with it if we think we have it?

This is the moment when we can determine if we are destined for greatness and notoriety or not. The very first thing I am going to say, is if you have deep icy/ cold inner thoughts of murder or mass genocide, put the book down and pick up the phone and call the emergency hotline in your area!

If your thoughts are that you have some deep unfulfilled passionate desire to be or do something great, then it is time you finish this book fast and start working on achieving that precise dream! Get a thought mode going that would enable you to step out from the pack and as that famous giant Nike says "Just Do It!" There are many of us who do not have that inner power in our "persona" on the surface but we do have a special power but we just are afraid to tap into it, this is the time to make every effort to work aggressively on warming your "persona" to the warmest you can and then some, in search of that place where you can truly take control of your own "persona" in such a way that you can live your life using your power over your "persona" to influence every living moment of your life so that your power and deeds influence all those you come in contact with. This is a state that is truly awesome and for absolute certain, you will be remembered by all who come into your presence. I must say that this power is incredibly strong, for most people, they do not even know that they have a "persona" so anyone who can not only be aware of it, but "walk the walk" so to speak in the complete knowledge of it's existence every hour of their awake lives and live to the absolute best that they can be in every scenario of their life, this is true control and it is living in "The Top Drawer" there is no better place to be other than heaven itself.

I think that throughout history there are very few people who have truly found that place, partially because most people just aren't aware of their "persona" for those who are, they have to make a conscious choice of self improvement in a way that far exceeds the commitment of a priest or a monk or nun, it is a commitment of making your life as completely rounded in the absolute best way possible in all aspects of one's life.

This involves control of ones temperament, ones thoughts, ones opinions of others, it involves taking control of ones habits ones life style ones outward presentation of demeanor, ones facial expressions, body language and learning to control ones feelings and outward emotions, it is an all encompassing spiritual and physical commitment which few choose to follow and many more don't care enough to look at.

No we cannot all be perfect, that is not it; we can strive for improvement in all these things, even if we try a little then we can try some more if we succeed and the very decision to do that makes us a better human being and that influences our "persona."

The "Top Drawer" is a dream situation, but we can always try to follow our dreams and the closer we get to achieve our dreams, the better we feel, and the better we feel, the better we appear to those who see us from the outside. It is the commitment we make and the willpower we use to carry it through that makes the difference between mediocrity and true success, this applies to life in general and should become if not already there, a mindset for all people.

The world we live in today is one that has no choice but to breed hatred and despair for many, there is poverty in extreme numbers, AIDS cases in millions, war for millions in active everyday life and religion has secularized itself to such an extent, it is a disgrace on those who lead the individual faiths to not put out their hands in friendship to those who would be their enemy just because they believe in God a different way. I placed John Paul II on the list above (I am not a Catholic) because he did put his hand out to other religions and had some success as a result of doing this. There needs to be a huge amount more of this done by others of the Jewish, Muslim, Buddhist, Christian etc, leaders they could create world peace by just living what they preach, goodness exists in almost all people with some exceptions but it is those with evil in their "personas" who are exerting minority influence on the masses, causing war, hunger, poverty, terrorism, you name it they seem to have the power. The truly orangey/red positive leadership "persona" who takes the bull by the horns in the religious community, can influence history and the world themselves by their actions, they just need to "Do It"! SOON!

Let me tell you a story from my own life about power and strength in a "Public Persona." Some time ago my wife and I and our children (now grown up) lived in Orange County, California. When we moved there, we had not really exercised our religious disposition in any way for years and it really hadn't bothered me much as I believed then that if you lived a good life that all would be o.k. in the next.

Anyway, we hit on hard times and I personally was challenged greatly to not only maintain my "persona" at an acceptable level in the family unit but also on a public level to maintain my ability to sell Real Estate. Anyway, the challenges were enormous and we were trying to weather a depression in the Real Estate market and survive. When I say survive, it got so bad that we lost everything, and every day was a steep slope of survival. One day I got up and was planning my day over a cup of tea and wondering where I was going to find the rent for my office which was late and threatening eviction, I believed if I kept the office going, things would change and we would have a way of making a recovery. I just could not imagine how I was going to pay it. I drove to work as usual and unlocked the door, as I opened the door I looked down and lying on the floor was a money order made out to my wife and me and it was for $1000 and inscribed at the bottom was a statement "Because God Loves You!" No name on it to tell me who gave it to us or any other way we could identify the donor. It was real and it was the exact amount that I was short to pay the rent. A miracle? I think so, whoever you are that did that incredibly warm and positive deed; it is appreciated always to this day by my wife and I.

My story continues: as a result of this deed and another incredible miracle that happened to us which I will tell on another occasion, we decided to go to church on an invite from a couple who were very close friends. The church was Saddleback church, the now famous Rick Warren ("The Purpose Driven Church" and the Purpose Driven life" books author) was the head pastor there and we found GOD again through his inspirational teachings of the bible, this was a time when I believe we were at tight quarters with one of those very gifted people. Rick Warren has the ability to convey the warmth of his "persona" through his teachings, he can make an audience of 3000 plus people feel like he is having a personal conversation with them, his gift is to be able to make one feel that his message is specifically for you and that is a powerful strength, it comes from within his "persona" which may well be guided by GOD himself. For those who have never heard Rick Warren speak, he is a gifted speaker and a truly inspirational one to listen to, and he has a "public persona" that is warm and positive in every way.

Rick Warren through his "public persona" and belief in GOD has built a congregation that is probably one of the largest in an individual church in the whole of the USA and he has created ministries that circumvent the globe helping in places of starvation, disease and poverty, he has influenced thousands of pastors and preachers to change the way they teach religion to a more modern-day level of understanding and in doing so, made it easier for people suffering from the pressures of life to find GOD. His "persona" is his projection system; his power is his belief in God, what a combination! I am proud to have met such a person who is so totally committed to his belief in himself, his wife and family and his life's purpose.

I think it is times when we are at our lowest that we are at our most vulnerable, and we have to hope that at these times good comes our way, because evil could be just as influential if we were to let it and I think that criminals are good examples of such influences taking control of the "persona".

The power of a "persona" to influence if used in a certain way is incredible. The question is can we all dig deep enough within our own "persona" to find such power? Yes I believe so. The problem is depth of commitment, and this is what this is all about .Are we committed to self-improvement enough to let it take control of all the negative influences within our "persona?"

When people say to you "have a nice day" does it mean any more to you than the words? It should mean a lot, because you should be living it anyway. The response should be "I am already thank you," how about you, are you having a great day?"

The inner power that we all possess is so influential to each and every one of us, I think sometimes we suppress it because we are intimidated by it and we are fearsome of allowing those powers to come out into the open for it might embarrass us or it might intimidate others or we might make a fool of ourselves if we demonstrate what mediocrity might call us to task on. The real truth is that if the powers are warm and non-confrontational and they are influential in a positive non-invasive way, it is good and should be exploited gently at first but with more liberal use as we see the results if they are having a good effect on those around us.

A wonderful experiment to use in company, try exercising your good influences on a group in gentle amounts, whether it be in raising the enjoyment level of the occasion spiritually for all you come in contact with, or use your own charisma to elevate the whole occasion on mass for all present, this could be by praising someone or by making a speech with some meaning to it that might individually affect all who listen, or perhaps by performing a selfless act that can be observed by all. This is just a starting place, as you get more proficient at projecting your power of influence, you need to create a plan of action with challenges that allow you to spread your wings and do it in a very meaningful way. Use your own special gifts as a person to enhance the success of your efforts both socially and at work.

You have to search deep to find those special attributes and as you search, you will find so many other good things that you never knew you possessed that can come into play in your goal to reach the "Top Drawer" it is so exciting, you have to try it!

Start simple and keep working at it, all the people I have listed above, started with a dream and went from there. Remember, this is only for good; the evil people listed above are there for illustration purposes only to show how bad a person can become if they choose to allow the devil inside them to take control and should not be copied.

You might also have noticed in my list of "personas" above that they are from all different career choices, religions, races, wealth and a whole lot more. In other words the "personas" that each of them possess or possessed were used in totally different ways, but nevertheless the "persona" that they have used in their life has influenced millions some over history and some in their own lifetime, either way, they have been a phenomenon in their lifetime. You can see that it is not what they did but how they influenced others that made them what they are, it is their "personas" that influenced all around them!

Good leaders make people feel that they're at the very heart of things, not at the periphery. Everyone feels that he or she makes a difference to the success of the organization. When that happens, people feel centered and that gives their work meaning.

Warren Bennis

Conclusion

I have written this book to help the many who seek a better self-image and lifestyle as you have read, my book is about how we all relate with each other; some relate easily and warmly and others have difficulty relating and do so by being cool and hard to understand. I believe that we are born with a basic metabolism of life and we all have a genetical makeup for our personality which if left untamed, becomes our personality and sometimes if tamed in the wrong or right way, is manipulated into being the way we are in the world around us.

I believe that we are all born different and we are all masters of our own destiny and identity. Quite simply, if we so choose, we can control our own demeanor as it affects the world around us and ourselves individually. I believe that we have enough power to control the disposition of others around us and the way they relate with us as a result of that power we assert on them. Have you ever noticed how people react to you when you are in a bad mood and generally cool disposition? Mostly they either get a serious look on their face or it can make them angry and aggressive. On the other hand have you noticed how they react when you are happy and joyous and emulate waves of warm feelings? They tend to want to ride your bandwagon and react in a warm and friendly way to you. Well that is what I why I wrote this book and I thank my upbringing for the experiences and observations I have revealed in the previous pages. I hope that if you are single, married, with kids or not, male or female, old or young, religious (any religion) or not, rich or poor, white, black, brown, yellow or green, that you will open your mind to the possibilities I have shared with you, and I hope I can inspire you to lead and enjoy a better, more aware life as a result of this reading experience.

Often we go about our daily lives paying attention to our busy timetable and the pressures that are dealt us in voluminous quantities by the way we live our lives. We often create bigger burdens on ourselves just by the way we treat others who live around us and with us. People react to us in ways that we don't even notice. Even as a six-month old baby we are influenced by those around us, our parents, their friends and other children. It is not really incomprehensible to realize that if our lives are so influenced by the company and relationships that we keep, that it is possible something within each and every one of us makes us emit an energy that can enable us, knowingly or not, to shape the relationships and interactions that we have with others in our every day lives.

During my life I have found that by studying fellow mankind in my every day life I have been able to find success in business, in my relationships with others, in sales and also in my private life. I have not as yet perfected my own "persona" but I do have a "Top Drawer," a wish list if you like. I have heroes and heroines in the "persona" realm who I aspire to improve to and hopefully one day surpass, and if I fail, it will not be because I gave up. The point of my book is that if you put it down after reading it to here and you feel that you have room for improvement in your own "persona" then I have succeeded.

My goal is to make the world a better place to live in and if my part is to help fellow mankind to be nicer to those around them and live a more considerate, less selfish, lifestyle and find a more spiritual side of themselves.

The tough part is, after you have read this book and you feel somewhat inspired to make good changes that you remain true to the challenge of making the changes. I have made suggestions in this book on how to attack issues in your life and how to deal with them; it is only my opinion and you can change anything you like. The key is that you learn a way to address those weakness and pains that affect your everyday life and be strong enough to put them behind you. It is imperative that you use a specific method of itemizing the issues and a specific way of closing the door on them. If you feel that you cannot do this, seek advice from a knowledgeable friend or specialist. Whatever you do, do something. To leave it festering will only allow it permission to stay inside your body and your life and that cannot happen if you want to truly make changes that will improve your life and the lives of those around you.

The idea of a "persona" temperature, color, electrical charge is in my opinion a wonderful way to illustrate the true inner being of one's soul and the illustration makes it very easy to assess on a regular/daily basis how we are doing. Use it: I LOVE it and I think you will also.

The book applies to all who would give it a try; it works and as I have stated so many times in the book, dish out immeasurable amounts of unconditional acts of LOVE. Don't be selfish, don't be verbally abusive, don't be concerned about what others are thinking and doing, don't be jealous. Always do the right thing, always be truthful, always try to smile, always turn the other cheek (unless there is no alternative!) and always show compassion.

Just live by the standards of how you would like others to treat you. The results will be astounding; your life will change and your LOVED ones will feel the warmth of your presence whenever you are around.

My LOVE to you all and may your "persona" glow warm/orangey/ red/ positive for the rest of your days. From here on it is up to you.

God Bless Life and the riches it bestows upon us all!

Roy Taylor

Above all else guard your heart, for it is the wellspring of life.

Proverbs 4:23